GREAT REVIEWS!

"It practically holds your hand with its
step-by-step itineraries."
—*Conde Nast's Traveler*

"...a new approach to seeing this great
and venerable city."
— *The Foot Loose Librarian*

"...the perfect solution for travelers
making brief stays in that wonderful town."
— *Star-Tribune, Minneapolis*

"...for travelers who don't have time to plan and
don't want to go on a group tour, who want hints
on seeing the city's famous sites as well as some
equally fascinating places that aren't as well known."
—*Associated Press*

"...a chatty, good-natured tone makes her book
a cheerful, helpful companion."
—*Davis Enterprise*

"...a coordinated way to do London in a short time,
with tours based on traveler interests,
hobbies or professions."
—*World News Features*

"...puts it all together for you
and plans your brief time
so that you won't miss a single feature."
— *Active Senior Lifestyles*

Also by Ruth Humleker:

New York for the
Independent Traveler*

*Winner of the Benjamin Franklin Award
for "best published travel book"
from Publishers Marketing Association

London

FOR THE INDEPENDENT TRAVELER

ON YOUR OWN,
SEE THE LONDON
YOU WANT TO SEE.
A STEP-BY-STEP GUIDE

RUTH HUMLEKER

MARLOR PRESS
Saint Paul, Minnesota

LONDON FOR THE INDEPENDENT TRAVELER

5th Edition
A MARLIN BREE BOOK

Copyright 1987, 1990, 1995, 1999, and 2005 by Ruth Humleker
Maps by Dick Humleker

Distributed by to the book trade in the USA
by Independent Publishers Group, Chicago
Printed in the United States of America

ISBN-10: 1-892147-10-6
ISBN-13: 978-1-892147-10-3

Library of Congress Cataloging-in-Publication Data

Humleker, Ruth
    London for the independent traveler : on your own, see the London you want to see : a step-by-step guide / Ruth Humleker. -- 5th ed. p. cm.
    Includes index.
    "A Marlin Bree book" -- T.p. verso
    ISBN 1-892147-10-6
    1. London (England) -- Guidebooks. I. Title

DA679.H86 2005
914.2104'86--dc22   2005051091

MARLOR PRESS, INC.
4304 Brigadoon Drive
Saint Paul, Minnesota 55126

CONTENTS

candle-lit dinners. No other city has more for travelers with romance in their souls – if they know where to look.

108 ROYAL LONDON

Fairy-tale turrets, knights in armor and banners billowing in the breeze – all part of the legends and history of royalty. Follow the track of royalty from Windsor Castle to Buckingham Palace. You can see magnificent sights and get a real feel for the extraordinary life of the royals in and near London.

126 IN THE FOOTSTEPS OF DIANA

You can visit some of the places made special by the late Princess Diana, from where she lived in her first apartment with her merry band of "Sloane Rangers" to her fabulous wedding at Westminster Abbey and her life as a Royal. Walk in her footsteps to some of her favorite places, including where she ate and where she shopped.

132 LITERARY LONDON

Trod the cobblestones where Shakespeare presented his plays; see where Rudyard Kipling wrote his famous works. This is your special guide to literary London – where almost every important writer in the English language has lived, worked, or studied. Hey, maybe a little of their luck will rub off on you.

154 MARINER'S LONDON

Take a boat ride down the Thames, visit a famous clipper ship. Re-live some of the romantic age of sail. See lots of boats. Visit historic waterfront taverns. You don't have to be a sailor to enjoy this colorful nautical outing.

172 SHOPPER'S LONDON

London is one of the greatest shopping centers in the world. Here's a wide swinging tour through the best of London's elegant, quaint, or just plain fun places to shop, organized by a veteran and loving shopper. Bring money.

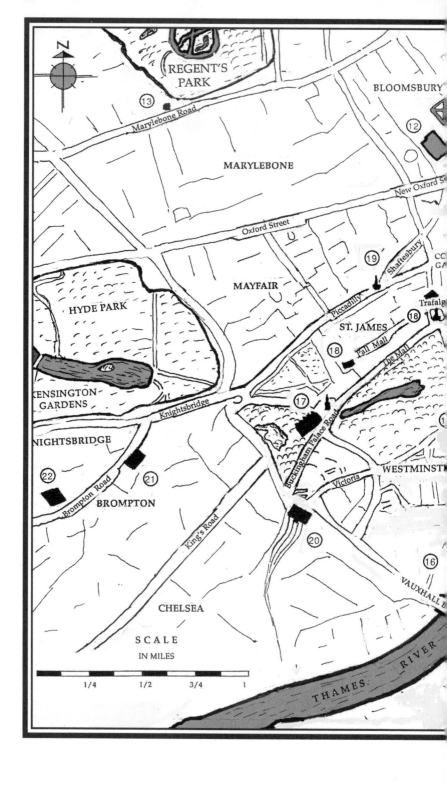

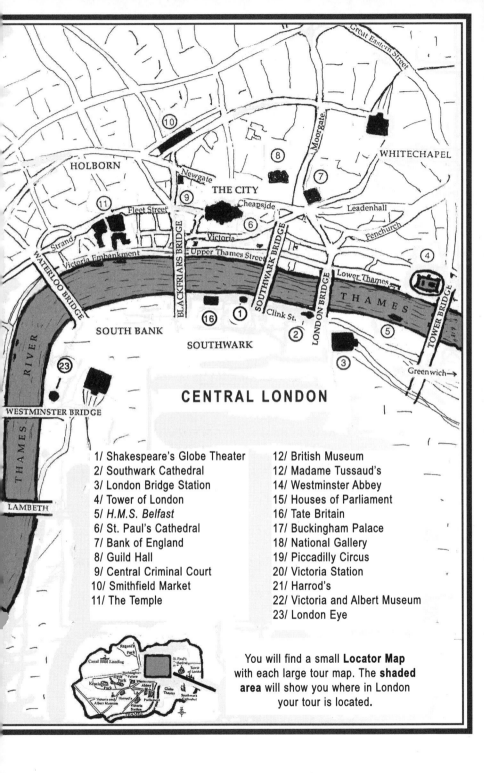

CENTRAL LONDON

1/ Shakespeare's Globe Theater
2/ Southwark Cathedral
3/ London Bridge Station
4/ Tower of London
5/ *H.M.S. Belfast*
6/ St. Paul's Cathedral
7/ Bank of England
8/ Guild Hall
9/ Central Criminal Court
10/ Smithfield Market
11/ The Temple

12/ British Museum
12/ Madame Tussaud's
14/ Westminster Abbey
15/ Houses of Parliament
16/ Tate Britain
17/ Buckingham Palace
18/ National Gallery
19/ Piccadilly Circus
20/ Victoria Station
21/ Harrod's
22/ Victoria and Albert Museum
23/ London Eye

You will find a small **Locator Map** with each large tour map. The **shaded area** will show you where in London your tour is located.

GUIDE TO LONDON
MAPS & FLOOR PLANS

London

FOR THE INDEPENDENT TRAVELER

Introduction:

HOW THIS BOOK
CAN HELP YOU

MOST GUIDEBOOKS give you information on restaurants, hotels, museums, parks and historical monuments, but they let you sort out your own tours. The result is often that you are at one end of town, with the next place you want to see at the other so you waste time and effort.

Other books feature walking guides, which in reality take too long and are too complex. These books can be useful for people who will be in London for weeks at a time, but are too detailed for the average visitor with only days to spend in this great city.

In this book, I try to assemble all the pieces of this traveler's jigsaw puzzle into chronological, geographical and special interest tours for the independent traveler.

Each day is arranged into a tour following a **special map**, so you can see at a glance where you are going and what you have left to do. I have a **timetable** and make specific recommendations so that, while you may not see everything, at least you will be seeing the **main features.**

MAJOR CHANGES have taken place during the past few years. A Millennium Commission coordinated plans and funding from the lottery proceeds and corporate sponsorships.

The centerpiece of their plans was the $1.24 billion Millennium Dome built on the site of the Greenwich Prime Meridian, widely accepted as a starting point for time keeping. Richard Rogers, architect for the Pompidou Center in Paris, designed the dome, a ring of steel masts supporting a roof 1,050 feet in diameter, covering 20 acres. At this point in time, the permanent use for this space is still under study. Christmas 2003 found it housing shops and other holiday events.

A Millennium Bridge now takes pedestrians across the Thames to the Tate Gallery's new national art gallery. The new Hungerford Bridge connects the Victoria Embankment with the south bank Jubilee Gardens and the amazing 450' high London Eye or as I call it, the gigantic Ferris Wheel.

The British Library is now located at St. Pancras railway station after its move from the British Museum. The British Museum was renovated by Sir Norman Foster with a gorgeous new Reading Room under a gigantic glass dome, plus many other changes.

A renovated Kensington Palace opened in the spring of 1998; the Courtauld Institute galleries reopened in the summer of 1998 in the Somerset House on The Strand; the Thomas Coram Foundation for children, under renovation, is currently on view only by special admission: Call 020 7841 3600.

The restaurant scene has exploded in London; there are more and more fascinating new places to eat. In addition to these walking tours, do invest in the Zagat Survey of London Restaurants; it is updated every year. Although I do select a number of restaurants for you to try as you walk these walks, I could not begin to cover the hundreds of places reviewed in the Zagat.

M Y GOAL IS TO MAKE EACH DAY as pleasant and inclusive as possible without exhausting either the traveler's body or pocketbook. You do that by traveling smarter, not harder. The result is that many travelers tell me they can do as much in three great days as most do in a week.

The chapters are arranged in **three-day tours,** since that is often the amount of time a visitor spends in London before renting a car and touring Britain or crossing the channel to Europe.

As you read, you'll probably find a **theme** that will interest you, whether it's Basic London, London for Romantics, Literary or Mariners London or even Children's London.

For example, my first plan is the **Basic Three Days in London.** This is for travelers who want to see all of London during their brief visit, and of course I want to help them see the major points of interest. They'll visit London's great attractions, including the Tower of London, St. Paul's Cathedral, Westminster Abbey, the Houses of Parliament and Big Ben, Buckingham Palace, the British Museum, Regent's Park and finally, they'll even take a boat trip down the Thames River to see the illuminated city. It's really maximum London in just three days.

ANOTHER TOUR I have designed is for **romantics**, which includes a visit to Mayfair and Shepherd's Market, an outdoor theatre production at Regent Park, a river trip down the Thames to Henry VIII's Hampton Court with its beautiful State Apartments and magnificent gardens, the charming shops along Piccadilly, Jermyn and St. James's streets; a picnic in St. James's lovely park, with groceries purchased at Fortnum and Mason's elegant store, a stop at the Queen's Gallery and a walk around Buckingham Place. The tour culminates with dinner at St. Katherine's Dock and the 700-year-old Ceremony of the Keys at the Tower of London.

Perhaps your interest is **Literary London**, which includes Southwark, where Chaucer and Shakespeare worked, Carlyle's and Dicken's fascinating houses, and the not-to be-forgotten Poet's Corner at Westminster Abbey. Mariner's London takes a voyage up the Thames to Greenwich to visit the famous clipper Cutty Sark, go aboard the H.M.S. Belfast, and take a ride on one of London's famous canal boats.

IF YOUR INTEREST IS GARDENING, **Gardener's London** is three days among the plants and flowers, featuring the world-famous Chelsea Flower Show with a side trip to the Chelsea Physic Garden. A day trip to the Royal Botanic Gardens (better known as the Kew Gardens), and the Syon House Garden, will be a gardener's delight.

There's even a **Children's London** so that travelers with children can have a special three days visiting the Tower of London, have a swim in the Serpentine in Kensington Gardens, ice skate at the Queen's Ice Skating Club, and take a canal boat ride on their way to the world-famous London Zoo.

That's just a sample. There are many places to go and see if you have a special interest. You can combine tours and days or turn them upside down. There is no reason an art lover could not combine a day from Art Lover's London, one from Gardener's London and one from Romantic London. In most instances that will work. Just be careful to notice opening and closing times of public buildings. The plans are arranged to accommodate those hours.

A S YOU FOLLOW the tour plans, try to stay on the **time schedule** if you want to see all the places recommended. I have walked all these tours at a moderate pace and they do work. This assumes, of course, that you will not loiter, drag your feet or become absolutely fascinated with some particular place. And of course you will. Don't worry about it. Just use these tours to help you steer your own course through London.

My rule of thumb regarding restaurants, pubs, shops or public buildings is that if it was not there for at least 100 years, I would not mention it. Not quite true, but close. There are no trendy fern bars in this book. Many of these places are located in central London and are convenient stops on more than one tour. They are also my favorites: restaurants and pubs which have never failed me; shops which provide attentive service and museums which are endlessly fascinating. I hope you find them so, too.

A VISITOR CAN HAVE IT ALL in London: sightseeing, shopping, art, gardens, parks, castles, good food and the best theatre in the world. It's all there for the taking.

This is my advice, with all my biases and loves and hates showing, but I think it can be your London, too. I hope so because I want you to love this city as much as I do.

Two hundred years ago Dr. Samuel Johnson said, "When a man is tired of London he is tired of life; for there is in London all that life can afford." It is still true.

Get your passport and plane ticket, pack your good manners and enthusiasm and tuck this book under your arm.

Bon Voyage!

PRACTICAL
INFORMATION

WHEN TO VISIT LONDON

TIPS ON FLYING

CUSTOMS & CURRENCY

MINIMIZING JET LAG

TRAVEL INTO LONDON

GETTING AROUND LONDON

THOSE WONDERFUL VISITOR CENTERS

THEATRE INFORMATION

ABOUT TIPPING

PRACTICAL
INFORMATION

L ONDON IS A LIVING, BREATHING, CHANGING CITY. This is important to remember because many of us tend to think of it as a
static museum city. I know I did for a long time.

I was annoyed when the Royal Mews were not open on a
Wednesday afternoon because the horses were at Windsor. I was
furious when I realized I could no longer get a clear look at St.
Paul's Cathedral as I walked up Ludgate Hill because an office
building blocked the view. I huffed and puffed my way around
Bankside's construction. I wanted it all to remain the way it was
when I first saw it. But it didn't and it won't.

Be prepared for such changes. Some may occur between the
time this book is written and when you take it with you on your
walks around London. The information is as accurate as possible,
but there will be changes.

TRAVEL SAFETY

T HE VERY IDEA of travel makes many people uncomfortable.
The first time I went to Europe it was like going to the moon.
The excitement of travel is usually accompanied by a certain
amount of anxiety.

Added to one's normal nervousness from tales about pickpockets, motorcycle gangs, muggers and now terrorists, it is no
wonder that travelers have second thoughts about going to new
places.

While the average tourist can do little to change the climate of our times, there are specific things you can do to look after yourself. To put it in perspective, you have more chance of hurting yourself in a car accident or even by falling in a bathtub, than you have in traveling about London, which has always been among the safest cities in the world.

Many tourists tend to travel in large tour groups, which are visible and tempting targets for all kinds of pickpockets and con artists. As an independent traveler, you will fit in more with the London scene by not becoming highly visible.

Avoid crowds, which pickpockets seem to work with great success.

Visit major sights early in the morning or late in the afternoon instead of mid-day, when tour groups are visiting. When possible, travel in the spring or fall instead of the busy, crowded summer months.

Dress down. Leave your gold chains, Rolex watches and diamonds at home.

Do not carry more money or traveler's checks than you need for the day. Do not put your wallet in your back pocket, with or without the ubiquitous rubber band. These pickpockets are good!

Be sensible. You wouldn't walk down a dark alley at home; don't do it abroad. Use your head and don't let a few strange sights or imposing buildings make you lose your common sense.

Airlines have instituted more stringent security check-in procedures and inspections. Get to the airport at least two hours ahead of your flight time; go through the security checks quickly and politely, so you are not in the unsecured part of the airline terminal any longer than necessary.

When possible, take non-stop flights to avoid sitting around in airports. Report suspicious behavior to airline personnel.

Do not carry anybody else's luggage aboard if that person is not traveling with you. Listen to the flight instructions. It is the sophisticated traveler who knows how to use the life jacket, if necessary, not the one who was too blase to pay attention to emergency directions.

WHEN TO VISIT

THE WEATHER may influence the time you choose to visit London. The temperature in winter is in the 40's, in spring the upper 50's, summer the mid 60's to low 70's, and fall in the low 60's. Those are all Fahrenheit temperatures.

Though it may rain mostly in the spring and winter, my fall trips have included many rainy days. If you just face the fact that it probably will rain no matter when you go, you'll be prepared.

August is London's busiest tourist month. Personally, I like to go in early spring and late fall in order to miss the bulk of the tourist travel.

But whatever your travel constraints, go whenever you can arrange it.

TIPS ON FLYING

ON A LONG FLIGHT, seat selection can make a big difference in your comfort. If I have a choice, I ask for a bulkhead seat. These are located on aisles and near the exit doors and have much more legroom because there is not a seat in front of them.

The disadvantages are that you often have people crossing in front of you and some of the seats near the doors are drafty. Personally, I put up with the disadvantages to get the legroom.

At the time you make your flight reservation, you can also order the special meal you want for dietary or religious reasons, such as vegetarian, kosher, diabetic, no or low salt, or fruit plates.

When you board, put your carry-on baggage in the overhead storage bins. Save your legroom.

This is a good time to get one of the small pillows, to tuck in the small of your back or for sleeping, and one of the blankets. If you choose, this is a good time to change your shoes for slippers and switch your jacket for a more comfortable sweater.

Listen to the flight instructions and keep your seat belt fastened. I loosen my belt but keep it buckled all the time I am in my seat. You never know when an unexpected air pocket or other emergency will occur. The flight crew does everything to warn you in advance, but most seasoned flyers just leave their belts secure during the trip.

And finally, remember to reconfirm your flight when you are ready to return home.

PASSPORT

A PASSPORT AND MONEY in some form are the two essentials for your trip. They won't let you out of the country without the passport and without money you aren't going very far, either. Contact the appropriate government agency to get passport applications and information.

Get your passport early, long before your trip, so you won't have to worry about it. In most countries, the best time to apply is between September and January. The heaviest demand is usually in March.

Once you have your passport, guard it with your life. Either photocopy the first two pages or write the number of your passport, date and place of issue on a piece of paper; keep it in a separate place. In case of loss this precaution will be useful in helping you secure a replacement. If your passport is lost, notify the police in London and your embassy. The embassy can issue a replacement or a temporary passport for the duration of your trip.

But do not lose it. Carry your passport with you or leave it in the locked safe in your hotel. Do not leave it in your room, even locked in your bag.

Incidentally, depending on the kind of hotel you stay in, check to be sure it has a safe and is not just tucking things underneath the counter.

CUSTOMS

I WILL NOT EVEN ATTEMPT to spell out the Byzantine custom regulations which change periodically. Write your Customs Service for their most recent publications concerning customs requirements.

I will add just one note, which you might otherwise overlook: Customs can impound (that means take and keep) counterfeit merchandise, including fake Gucci bags or shoes, imitation Vuitton luggage, and other bootlegged merchandise.

This is done to protect the trademarks of a foreign country, but it can come as a shock to travelers who thought they had made some great buys.

CURRENCY

EVERYONE YOU TALK TO will give you different information on how to take your money abroad. So take my advice with a grain of salt and decide how you will be most comfortable. I will just tell you what I have learned and how I do it.

It took me a while to understand that money is a commodity that is bought and sold like anything else. Since banks handle so much money, they can usually give the best deals.

First, I locate a bank at home which has an international department and buy a small amount of British currency before departing. This is for immediate expenses, such as taxis, tipping or bus tickets.

If you are not near such an international center, don't worry. London airports have exchange desks in their air terminals. I advise using the local bank because it saves time on your arrival.

When the money market is volatile and the rates are changing rapidly, the following tips may prove useful:

If the dollar is rising, don't change dollars into pounds ahead of time and don't buy traveler's checks in the currency of the country. Don't change all your money into pounds when you arrive.

Use your credit cards for payment. If the dollar is falling, exchange your dollars as soon as possible or buy your traveler's checks in the currency of the country.

Plan to take some of your own currency in small denominations. It can come in handy both in London and when you return home. I use traveler's checks. Many banks provide their customers with these, commission free. It is possible to get your traveler's checks in British currency, which eliminates changing money twice. While convenient, it may not be the best buy.

Credit cards are accepted most places. Just remember, your purchases are charged at the prevailing rate when the merchant bills your credit card company, not at the moment of purchase. This can make a big difference in a fluctuating currency market.

When changing money in London, always go to a bank for the best rate. Even then you may want to check more than one bank to find the best rate. Ask what the bank is adding as a service charge. It can vary several pounds.

A warning: do not exchange money at the 24-hour credit exchanges. Their rates may be competitive but they can legally add a service charge.

Automated Teller Machines (ATMs) are available all over London, including Plus, Cirrus and other networks. Check with your bank regarding international withdrawal fees, which are often higher than domestic. Also ask if your PIN code needs to be reprogrammed for use in London.

The money you receive from a London ATM will be in local currency. The rate of exchange will be as good or better than what you would receive at a hotel or airport money counter.

Best advice: Exchange only as much as you expect to spend; use traveler's checks, which are insured if lost or stolen; and have enough British currency when you arrive to cover immediate expenses.

Remember to record the serial numbers of your traveler's checks and mark off the ones you use. Keep this record in a separate place, for it is important to have these numbers if you lose the checks.

British currency is in the form of pound sterling: each pound contains 100 pence. Spend some time before you leave home or in your hotel room studying and getting acquainted with the currency. You do not want to be flashing around your money in public.

A little hand converter is very handy, but you really do not need it unless you are traveling to a number of countries with a variety of currency.

And one final piece of advice: Everyone will tell you that no one will accept a personal check. I carry some with me and they have come in remarkably handy; indeed, many merchants and hotels have been delighted to take them.

DON'T LEAVE HOME WITHOUT

WHAT ELSE should you take, now that you have your passport and money? The most important things to me are an adventurous spirit, good manners and a positive attitude. Good manners and enthusiasm cover a multitude of evils. Remember that you probably will find pretty much what you expect, so expect the best, try the new, laugh at the snags, and enjoy.

Other than the all-important mental conditioning, here are some suggestions to make you a better and more comfortable traveler.

First of all, the more experienced the traveler, the less he or she carries. Ask any bellboy or porter. Everything in life is a trade-off, so why should travel be any different?

Make up your mind whether you want to see or be seen. Best advice: take half of what you think you will need.

Be sure to take any necessary medications on the plane with you; do not pack them. It is also sensible to take a copy of your prescriptions, just in case you need a refill. Take your prescriptions in their original, labeled bottles for identification going through customs.

If you have any physical conditions which might demand medication, take it with you. If you wear glasses or contact lenses, an extra pair may come in very handy.

I am not going to give you a list of clothes. This choice is very personal, and how do I know whether you wear pants or skirts or shirts or turtlenecks?

Just some broad observations: Color coordinate. Lay your clothes on your bed and match the colors of your shirts and skirts or pants with your shoes and scarves or ties. Remember clothes can be washed, thrown away or purchased in London.

Two absolute essentials for London: a light raincoat and a folding umbrella. I never leave my hotel or apartment in London without a folding umbrella in my bag. You can almost bet it will rain sometime during the day.

I suggest a light raincoat because I dress in layers: a cotton shirt, cardigan and coat. As the day goes on, I can peel or add clothes.

My feet are my number one priority. Take comfortable, well-broken-in shoes. Here is where style goes overboard and comfort wins. I use lambs wool to pad tender spots on my feet, wear heavy socks in my clunky tie shoes with non-slip crepe soles. Needless to say I wear pants to disguise my less-than-chic foot fashion. The lightweight running shoes are wonderful.

I do not take very dressy clothes. A silk shirt or a black cashmere sweater will take a woman almost anyplace. Grey slacks and a blazer will work for a man.

Of course I have a few idiosyncrasies. I add a flat-folded nylon suitcase for the extra things I buy.

In addition to the regular toiletries, I add soap and a washcloth, since some of the less-than-three-star hotels I stay in do not provide them; a universal bath plug for the same reason; band aids; and some kind of medication in tablet form for stomach distress. I know you can buy it there, but when I am in trouble, it is usually three o'clock in the morning.

I also take small packets of tissues, which can be used as toilet paper in an emergency.

IMPORTANT: Though you have carefully packed your bags, there are still some items you want to keep on or near you at all times. In your purse, carry-on bag, on your person or a combination of these, take your passport, currency, tickets, credit cards, glasses, medications, folding slippers, and trail mix, chocolate or whatever you like for snacks, in case the plane is delayed and you cannot get food. Never check anything essential in your check-in luggage.

LUGGAGE

B ASICALLY there are just three types of suitcases: hard, made-of-metal or plastic for rock stars and photographers; soft-sided with a rigid frame; and soft with no frame. What you gain in protection, you pay for in weight.

My advice: The best suitcase is the least suitcase. If you use vinyl or nylon, check on its durability and seams. Make sure it cannot be punctured and that it is as rainproof as possible. Almost nothing is completely waterproof since moisture can come in through zippers and other minute openings.

Luggage is a personal thing, so in determining your needs, look carefully and check prices. Just remember, you have to carry it.

Personalize your bag with colored tape or any other device for identification purposes. In the luggage line, all bags begin to look alike.

Put tags with your name, home address and destination inside and outside your bag. The sticky tags available from airlines work fine inside the bags. Your business card will fit in some luggage tags.

Some tags are covered to avoid easy identification by anyone but the owner. Remove any old tags. Give up the appearance of being a world traveler to avoid confusing the already baffled handlers.

Check baggage allowance, both weight and size. Usually two bags per person are free. Remember: Traveling light is the next best thing to having someone carry your bag.

PHOTOGRAPHY

WHILE WE ARE talking about what to bring to London, just a word about cameras and photography.

You probably have your favorite cameras and other photographic equipment. If you are not a fine photographer, let me suggest investing in some of the throw-away cameras, particularly the panoramic ones. They are lightweight, flexible and take some remarkable images. I particularly recommend them for your children: one for each child, please.

An important notice: The equipment that checks for bombs and other prohibited items also lays stripes on photographic film packed inside bags, according to the Federal Aviation

Administration and the manufacturer. Do not put undeveloped film in checked baggage.

According to the Photographic and Imaging Manufacturers Assn., the x-ray machines that scan carry-on luggage put out far less energy than the new bag scanners for check-on luggage.

Other suggestions: Put all film in a lead laminated film pouch, available at most camera stores.

Another option is to buy film when you reach your destination and have it developed before you leave for home.

HELP ASSURE ARRIVAL OF BAGGAGE

ONE GOOD WAY to insure the arrival of your luggage, in addition to your identification tags and removal of old tags, is to check in early. Double check the tag which the airline puts on your bag and don't be afraid to ask questions.

When you arrive, go directly to the baggage claim area to pick up your bags. In the unlikely event your bags do not arrive, report the loss immediately to the airline baggage office. Check the airline's limit of liability printed on the back of your ticket. Remember the liability is per passenger, not per bag.

You hear about the lost bags; you do not hear about the hundreds of thousands of bags which arrive safely, on time and in the right place.

JET LAG

THERE HAVE BEEN whole books written on how to avoid jet lag. My advice is fairly simple: Eat and drink lightly for a few days before you leave, and especially during your flight. Go easy on alcoholic drinks or avoid them altogether at this time.

Try to get some sleep during your flight. Take it easy on your arrival day. Don't plan to attend the theatre on your first night; you will probably doze off during the first act.

And synchronize your body clock with the local time as soon as possible.

ARRIVAL AND TRAVEL INTO LONDON

THE TWO MAIN airports in London are Heathrow and Gatwick. All charter flights fly to Gatwick, which prides itself on fast baggage reclaim. It has a little lounge near the escalators which lead to the baggage hall. This lounge is equipped with TV sets which announce the arrival of baggage.

Free baggage carts and the porters in brown uniforms are there to help you. If you need to change money, look for the currency exchange window.

You can take a bus or a very expensive cab ride the 25 miles into London, but the Gatwick Express train is by far the most sensible way to go to the center of London.

As soon as you pick up your bags and go through passport control, take an escalator downstairs to the train platform. The express trains leave for Victoria Station in London every 15 minutes during the day and every hour at night. At this writing, the charge is about $18 (First Class is about $28) for adults, half price for children 5 to 15; children under 5 ride free. The ride takes about half an hour from the airport to Victoria.

The Flightline Bus 777 leaves every half hour during the day; the fare is about $12 and it takes about an hour into the city.

Heathrow, the world's busiest international airport, has a three-story terminal complete with its own subway station on London Transport's Piccadilly Line. It handles incoming and outgoing passengers on different floor levels, which speeds up the handling of passengers and baggage.

Heathrow Express, is a 100-mile-per-hour rail link between the airport and Paddington Station in London. This trip should take about 15 minutes. Tickets are about $21. Children under 15 are free when with an adult.

The 50-minute underground subway (which I do not recommend for the tired traveler) ride costs about $7; the Airbus takes about an hour and costs approximately $10.

TRAVELING IN LONDON

THE BEST WAY to get around in London is on foot. When crossing the street, remember that London traffic moves the reverse of traffic in most other countries.

The British have tried to make it easier and safer for you by markings, *Look Right* and *Look Left,* on the street, near the curbs. They must have been losing too many of us. Be careful. It is hard to get used to looking the "wrong way" for cars and buses.

Pedestrians also are provided right of way in areas designated by white stripes. Be careful because while cars almost always stop, bicycles and motorcycles often do not.

The British also help walkers with their stop-and-go lights. The green walk light shows a little walking green man; the red stoplight shows a little red man standing still.

And finally, look for the pedestrian underground walkways that are provided at many of the busiest intersections, such as the entry to the subways. They are well marked, indicating exactly which way to go to arrive at the side of the road you are trying to reach, and can be real lifesavers.

The next best way around is the Underground or subway, known affectionately as the Tube. Get a Tube map. It is color-coded and very easy to read and use. The maps are posted in every underground station as well as in the trains themselves.

You can buy a "Go As You Please" ticket for use on any underground or bus for three, four, seven or fourteen days. This ticket is cheaper and easier to use than the single tickets, since you do not have to stand in line to buy one for each trip or worry about the right change.

If you will be in London for a week, buy a Zone 1 ticket, which will enable you to go anywhere in Central London on a tube or bus.

The tube runs from 5:30 a.m. to midnight and from 7:30 a.m. on Sunday to midnight.

The subways are built deep underground and have enormously long escalators that take you from the bowels of the earth to ground level. Stand to the right on them to let people in a hurry pass you. A few stops, such as the one at Russell Square, use an elevator to take you topside.

Buses are more complicated, but seeing London from the top of a double decker bus is worth figuring it out. Or just get on one and ride around a bit.

Do avoid rush hours; they are horrendous. Bus stops are marked by red signs with the word: *Request* in white letters.

Buses do not automatically stop; hail them by extending your arm. When you want to get off, ring the bell well in advance.

Or, you can always hail one of London's 13,500 cabs. London's boxy black cabs are as much a part of this city as the Tower of London or Westminster Abbey. All you have to do is wave your arm.

If the Taxi For Hire sign is illuminated, the cab is available. Most cabs cruise, although they often line up around hotels.

If you need to pre-book a cab, call ComputerCab (730-3450) run by the Licensed Taxi Drivers' Association. You pay for the distance the driver travels to you, up to a maximum of 1 pound, 20 pence.

THE CHUNNEL

THE EUROSTAR high-speed train travels through the 31-mile long tunnel underneath the English Channel from Waterloo station in London to either Gare du Nord in Paris or Gare du Midi in Brussels in a little better than three hours.

The Chunnel, as it is affectionately known, actually consists of three tunnels, two for trains and a service tunnel in between for emergencies and maintenance.

You can drive your car onto a train at one end and drive off Le Shuttle at the other. This $13.5 billion miracle was built entirely by private enterprise.

The trains leave every hour and provide first premium, first class and standard class seating. In addition to London, Paris and Brussels, Eurostar also serves Ashford, Calais-Frethun, Lille, Disneyland Paris and seasonal service to the Alpine towns of Moutiers and Bourg St. Maurice.

Check for the current fares with your travel agency or on the Internet or at Eurostar.com. There are usually some special rates for various times of the year or for particular categories of travel.

VISITOR CENTERS

THE LONDON TOURIST BOARD maintains information offices at Victoria Station, Liverpool Street Underground Station, Heathrow Airport, Waterloo International Terminal, Canary Wharf, Greenwich and Islington.

The British Travel Center at 12 Regent St., Piccadilly Circus, is open Monday through Friday from 9:30 a.m. to 6:30 p.m.; Saturday and Sunday from 10 a.m. to 4 p.m.

THEATRE INFORMATION

YOU CAN ORDER theatre tickets before you leave home through your travel agent or booking agents, or you can get them after you arrive, through your hotel, bookers or from the individual box offices.

Just like home, you will pay more buying through the hotel or booking agent. Box offices often do not answer their phones, so you best go directly to the theatre.

For tickets and information before you go, contact Global Tickets/Keith Prowse, 234 W. 44th St., Suite 1000, New York, N.Y. 10036. Telephone: 1-800-223-6108 or in New York: 212-398-4175; Fax 212: 302-4251. They will mail tickets to your home or fax you a confirmation and leave your tickets at the box office. The usual booking and handling fee is 20 percent added to the price of the ticket.

After you arrive in London, try the Society of London Theatre's discount ticket booth in Leicester Square. Tickets are available for some shows at half price plus a service charge. Tickets are limited to four per person and are sold only on day of performance. Credit cards are not accepted. Open Monday -

Saturday from 2:30 p.m. to 6:30 p.m. except on Sunday and matinee days when they are open from noon to 6:30 p.m.

Beware of unscrupulous ticket scalpers and pickpockets near this booth.

When ordering, note that the expensive seats are in the Stalls and Dress Circle, the less expensive ones in the Upper Circle and the cheapest seats in the Gallery. In hot weather avoid the Upper Circle seats, which are in the top balcony, except at the National and Barbican theatres, which have air conditioning.

Latecomers are not admitted until the end of the first act; be on time or you will find yourself watching Act One on closed circuit television in the foyer. Theatre programs are not free; they usually charge 60 to 80 pence. Theatres do provide cast lists free of charge, however.

Check newspapers and the publication, London Theatre Guide, which you can get at the air terminals, theatre booking offices and most hotels, to find out what is playing where.

My only advice is to consider a performance by the Royal Shakespeare Company, still part time at the Barbican Center, as well as a show at the National Theatre. Incidentally, the National Theatre has guided backstage tours at 10:15 a.m., 12:30 and 5:30 p.m. The 5:30 p.m. tour is convenient since it is just before performance time.

Most evening performances begin at 7:30 or 8 p.m; matinees usually on Wednesday, Thursday or Saturday at 1 or 1:30 p.m. Some theatres have early Saturday evening performances at 5 or 6 p.m.

One last tip. Almost all theatres have bars in the foyers. If you want a drink during the interval (intermission) you can order in advance, as you arrive at the theatre. You will find your drink placed on a table or ledge with your name on a slip of paper, waiting for you at intermission. It is a nice way to avoid the crush of people trying to get a drink.

One warning: drinks at these bars tend to be expensive and luke-warm.

OPENING TIMES

THE FOLLOWING are the open hours of some of the most wide-ly visited places in London.

Banks: Monday - Friday 9:30 a.m. to 3:30 p.m.

Pubs: Hours since 1988: 11 a.m. to 11 p.m., Monday to Saturday; noon to 3 p.m. and 7 to 10:30 p.m. on Sunday. Opening hours are often at the discretion of the owners.

Restaurants: Generally serve from 12:30 to 2:20 p.m. and 7 to 10:30 p.m

Shops: Monday - Saturday 9 a.m.to 5:30 p.m.

TELEPHONES

LOCAL CALLS are never free. Ask your hotel what they charge. DO NOT MAKE LONG DISTANCE PHONE CALLS FROM YOUR HOTEL ROOM. The surcharges can be astro-nomical.

The Post Office has the Westminster International Telephone Bureau at 1 Broadway, near St. James tube stop. It is open from 9 a.m. to 5:30 p.m. every day. They can help you call overseas.

HELPFUL TELEPHONE NUMBERS

IF YOU NEED **Directory Assistance**, Dial 142 for London, 192 for the rest of Britain.

If you need the **Operator**, Dial 100

American Express, 6 Haymarket (0171) 930 - 4411 M - F: 9 a.m. - 5:30 p.m.; Sat: 9 a.m. - 4 p.m.

Doctorcall, a service directing callers in London to a physician: 900-1000. Open 24 hours every day of the year. The doctor's standard consultation fee is reasonable.

Weather Forecast: (0171) 922-8844

Time: 123

Heathrow Airport: (0181) 759-4321 for flight information

Gatwick Airport: (0129) 353-5353 for flight information

TIPPING

TIPPING should be considered on the same basis in London as it is in your own country. You might want to remember what the word Tips meant originally: To Insure Prompt Service. So tip the 10 to 20 percent you would anywhere.

Just one piece of advice: A service charge of 10 to 15 percent is often added to your bill. No extra tipping is necessary in that event, so check your bill carefully.

VAT (VALUE ADDED TAX)

ENGLAND has a complicated Value Added Tax of 17 1/2 percent on purchases. However there exists something called the Personal Export Scheme, which exempts visitors from paying if the object is to be carried out of the country.

You need to show your passport and sometimes your return ticket to the shopkeeper, who will give you a VAT relief form to fill out. This completed form and the purchased goods must be presented to a Customs Officer in the VAT booth at the airport as you leave the country. You can then send the approved form back to the shopkeeper who will return your 15 percent.

This is a complicated and unwieldy operation. Hand carrying the goods through customs is only half the problem; cashing the checks often results in a loss, depending on the exchange rate and service charges. I recommend this scheme only in the event you make a substantial purchase and then only if you are willing to carry the object through customs.

For information, call 071-928-3344.

FOR UP TO DATE INFORMATION

READ ANY of London's newspapers or weekly publications such as Where, Time Out or City Limits.

DRUGS

DO NOT ATTEMPT to carry any form of illegal drugs in or out of the country. The United Kingdom, along with most countries, takes a very dim view of this kind of undertaking. Jail terms of five years for possession of cannabis and seven years for heroin or LSD possession would extend your trip, but in very unpleasant surroundings.

ON YOUR OWN:
SEE THE LONDON
YOU WANT TO SEE

BASIC THREE DAYS IN LONDON
ART LOVER'S LONDON
ROMANTIC LONDON
ROYAL LONDON
IN THE FOOTSTEPS OF DIANA
LITERARY LONDON
MARINER'S LONDON
SHOPPER'S LONDON
GARDENER'S LONDON
LEGAL LONDON
AUTHOR'S FAVORITE THREE DAYS
LONDON'S CEMETERIES

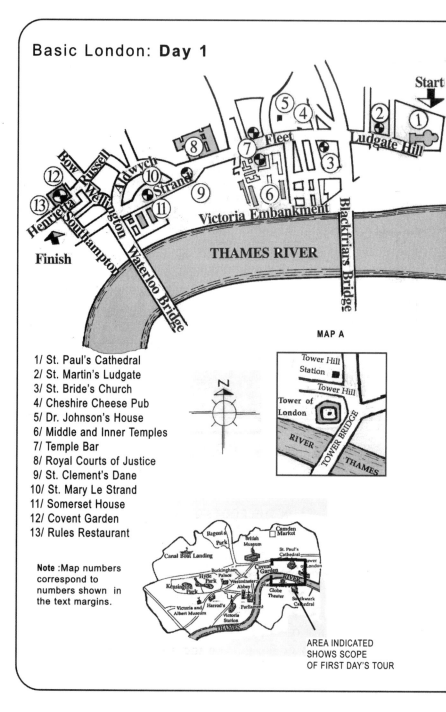

Basic London: Day 1

Start

Ludgate Hill

Fleet

Strand

Adwych

Bow

Russell

Wellington

Henrietta

Southampton

Waterloo Bridge

Victoria Embankment

Blackfriars Bridge

THAMES RIVER

Finish

1/ St. Paul's Cathedral
2/ St. Martin's Ludgate
3/ St. Bride's Church
4/ Cheshire Cheese Pub
5/ Dr. Johnson's House
6/ Middle and Inner Temples
7/ Temple Bar
8/ Royal Courts of Justice
9/ St. Clement's Dane
10/ St. Mary Le Strand
11/ Somerset House
12/ Covent Garden
13/ Rules Restaurant

Note : Map numbers
correspond to
numbers shown in
the text margins.

MAP A

Tower Hill
Station

Tower Hill

Tower of
London

RIVER

TOWER BRIDGE

THAMES

N

Regent's
Park

Camden
Market

British
Museum

St. Paul's
Cathedral

Tower
London

Canal Boat Landing

Buckingham
Palace

Covent
Garden

RIVER

Hyde
Park

Westminster

Kensington
Park

Abbey

Globe
Theater

Southwark
Cathedral

Harrod's

Parliament

Victoria and
Albert Museum

Victoria
Station

THAMES

AREA INDICATED
SHOWS SCOPE
OF FIRST DAY'S TOUR

BASIC
THREE DAYS
IN LONDON

The "most" London
you can do in a short time

THE BASIC THREE DAYS in London tour is for visitors to the city who are absolutely, positively certain they will never come back. Probably not true, but that is what they think. Tours in other chapters are planned for people with special interests, but this one is for the generalist who wants a sense of this great city in a few short days.

DAY 1

Highlights: Tower of London and the Ceremony of the Keys, St. Paul's Cathedral, Cheshire Cheese Pub and Covent Garden.

Reservations: Ceremony of the Keys at the Tower of London. Write Ceremony of the Keys, Waterloo Block, Tower of London, London, England, EC3N 4AB, for free tickets, well in advance of your visit to London. Indicate number of tickets and date desired and alternate dates. Include a stamped, self-addressed envelope (British stamps only) or two International Reply coupons. Rules Restaurant for dinner, 35 Maiden Lane. Telephone 020 7836-5314.

MORNING

DEPENDING ON THE LOCATION OF YOUR HOTEL, either take a cab or the tube to the **Tower of London.** The closest tube stop is Tower Hill. As you leave the under-

**MAP
A**

ground station, walk toward the street separating you from the Tower.

As you reach the sidewalk, you will find a stairway immediately on your left leading to the pedestrian underpass, which will take you safely under a very busy street to the Tower side. It is a short walk to the Tower. Try to get there when it opens at 9 a.m., before the tour buses arrive.

SEE TOWER OF LONDON DETAIL MAP

As you cross the moat leading to the Tower, glance down to see the green grass growing where water used to flow. Several years ago, palace authorities found it necessary to drain the foul-smelling water.

During the moat restoration, workers found surprising archeological remains: the most important being the Henry III gateway and the bridge that led to it. By matching rings of the timbers to climate data, scientists were able to link the remains to Henry's reign from 1216 - 1272. Other finds included a wicker fish trap, pottery, pipes and the old moat.

The 800-year-old **Tower of London** is the most important castle in England and the oldest continuously occupied, fortified building in Europe. It overlooks the Thames River and was intended to deter attackers from the river and to intimidate rebellious Londoners. Its 20 towers and 18 acres have held a mint, an observatory, a menagerie in the appropriately named Lion's Tower, an arsenal and a state prison.

Sir Walter Raleigh was held in the Bloody Tower for 13 years and it was here that the alleged murders of the little princes by Richard III took place in 1483.

The exteriors of many of the buildings are modern restorations but blend in wonderfully with the old fronts.

Walk from the entrance directly to the **Jewel House,** which contains the Crown Jewels and other royal regalia. If you arrive early, there should not be long waiting lines or queues, as they call them in London.

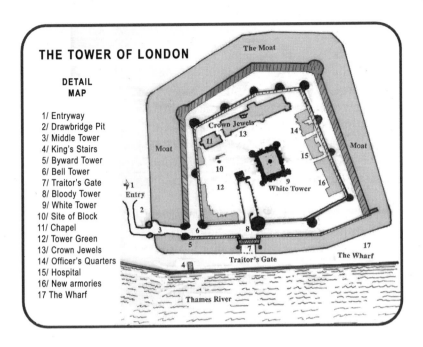

THE TOWER OF LONDON

DETAIL MAP

1/ Entryway
2/ Drawbridge Pit
3/ Middle Tower
4/ King's Stairs
5/ Byward Tower
6/ Bell Tower
7/ Traitor's Gate
8/ Bloody Tower
9/ White Tower
10/ Site of Block
11/ Chapel
12/ Tower Green
13/ Crown Jewels
14/ Officer's Quarters
15/ Hospital
16/ New armories
17 The Wharf

A moving platform keeps the crowds progressing, but you will have plenty of time to see the wonderful jewels, many of them so large it is hard to believe they are real. Be sure to especially notice Queen Victoria's Imperial State Crown, with the Star of Africa cut from the Cullinan Diamond, and the Crown of Queen Elizabeth (consort of George VI) set with the 108-carat Koh-i-Noor diamond. My favorite is Queen Victoria's little crown which she wore for less important occasions and which was not so heavy for her small head. It is a human touch among the glittering array of royal trappings.

After you leave the Jewel House, walk across the green and back near the entrance where you can join one of the Beefeater' Tours. These men are really Yeoman Warders, an order founded in 1485; 39 guard the tower and guide visitors. I will not recommend many guided tours, but this is a special mini-one. It will enable you to see and learn more in a brief period of time than you could do on your own. Be prepared to tip your guide as he leaves you, usually at the Chapel Royal of St. Peter ad Vincula where two of Henry VIII's wives, Anne Boleyn and Catherine Howard, are buried.

As you walk around you probably will see the ravens; the Crown protects and supplies them with food. It is said that the fall of the British Empire will occur if they ever leave the Tower. In order to provide double insurance, their wings are clipped.

NOW ON TO **St. Paul's Cathedral.** Either take a cab from the entrance of the Tower or tube to St. Paul's Station. I recommend a cab for this short trip since the tube ride involves a change of stations and is a bit awkward. Ask the driver of your nice black London cab to drive you through The City, the financial center of London, past the Bank of England and the Stock Exchange.

St. Paul's Cathedral is architect Sir Christopher Wren's masterpiece. Its dome is second in size only to that of St. Peter's, in Rome, after which it was modeled. Admission charged Monday through Saturday, 8:30 a.m. to 4 p.m. No sightseeing Sunday, services only. As you walk through its imposing doors, turn left.

All Souls Chapel, the first you will see on your left (North Aisle), contains a monument to World War I leader Field Marshal Earl Kitchener.

SEE ST. PAUL'S CATHE- DRAL DETAIL MAP

Further along the North Aisle is the Duke of Wellington's elaborate monument. Statues of Sir Joshua Reynolds and Dr. Samuel Johnson were hit by a bomb in 1941 and were refurbished in 1962.

Take time to examine the **Great Dome**, which rises 218 feet above the floor. The 62,000-ton dome appears to be suspended in mid-air, despite the fact it is supported by eight piers with Corinthian capitals that are buttressed by four huge supports.

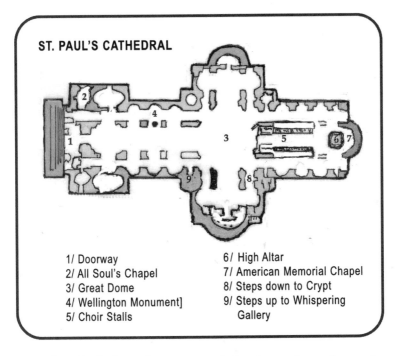

ST. PAUL'S CATHEDRAL

1/ Doorway
2/ All Soul's Chapel
3/ Great Dome
4/ Wellington Monument]
5/ Choir Stalls

6/ High Altar
7/ American Memorial Chapel
8/ Steps down to Crypt
9/ Steps up to Whispering
  Gallery

Directly below the center of the dome is a plaque to Sir Winston Churchill; another plaque here contains Wren's epitaph, If you seek his monument, look around (Si Monumentum requiris, circumspice for you Latin scholars).

Move up and around the choir stalls to see the carvings by Grinling Gibbons (you will hear his name when you see fantastic carvings throughout England) and the gorgeous wrought iron sanctuary gates by Jean Tijou.

You now will be behind the main altar in the **American Chapel** (formerly the Jesus Chapel), which contains an American Memorial to the 28,000 Americans based in England who were killed during World War II. Each day a page is turned in a huge book containing the names of the fallen. In one small corner of the memorial you can still see a hole left by one of the bombs. It is a very moving experience to stand quietly in this place.

In the **South Choir Aisle**, you will see the bizarre statue of the poet and Dean of St. Paul's, John Donne, wrapped in his funeral shroud. It serves to reinforce the story that Donne occasionally slept in his coffin. This is the only monument from the old church that survived the Great Fire.

As you leave the South Choir Aisle, you will see the entrance to the **Crypt.** Here you will find the tomb of Sir Christopher Wren, with the original tombstone containing the famous epitaph you saw earlier on the main floor of the Abbey; Wellington's tomb; the painters' corner with graves of J.M.W. Turner, Sir Joshua Reynolds, Sir John Millais and the American Benjamin West; and the tomb of Admiral Lord Nelson.

Go up the stairs to the south aisle, where you will find the entrance to the galleries, all 627 steps of them. You might want to climb the first 259 steps to the **Whispering Gallery,** where you can hear whispers from one side of the dome to the other. You must walk up 542 steps for the magnificent view from the Golden Gallery at the very top of the dome, but I do not recommend the whole climb unless you are in great aerobic shape. You are now back at the main entrance and ready to leave the Abbey.

NOON

B Y NOW you must be starved. As you walk down Ludgate Hill, turn and look back at St. Paul's to admire its magnificent exterior. Ludgate Hill becomes Fleet Street as you pass under the Holborn Viaduct (a 1/4 mile connection between Holborn Circus and Newgate Street). You will pass **St. Martin Within Ludgate**, a church rebuilt by Wren.

Look ahead of you, across Fleet Street and to your left, to see the soaring steeple of **St. Bride's Church.** A local baker took his inspiration for what is now our traditional wedding cake from that spire. St. Bride's was burned out during the air raid (Blitz) in 1940 but was rebuilt by 1957.

After crossing Shoe Lane, look for a narrow opening on your right. The overhead sign, which says Wine Office Court, leads the way to **Ye Olde Cheshire Cheese**, a ④ charming and popular tavern, rebuilt in 1667. It is said that Dr. Johnson and Boswell as well as Oliver Goldsmith were regular visitors.

A S YOU ENTER the low-ceilinged, smoky inn with its sawdust-covered floor, chances are you will be seated in the dining room to your left, at long tables with other people. There is often a fire burning in an open fireplace in the dining area. The two favorite items on the menu are roast beef and Yorkshire pudding, or steak and kidney pie. To your right is a small, noisy and crowded bar with tiny tables. If the weather is nice, you are apt to see people standing outside the tavern, drinking large mugs of ale or bitters. Ask to see the wine vaults in the basement. If they are not too busy, they will walk you down the narrow steps into the cellar with its wine storage and private rooms for entertaining.

Dr. Samuel Johnson's House is located just a few ⑤ steps beyond in Gough Square. Open Monday through Saturday, 11 a.m. to 5:30 p.m.

AFTERNOON

W ALK WEST on Fleet Street: on your left, across the street, you will see little entrances to **The Temple**, ⑥ the name for both the **Inner and Middle Temple**, two of the Inns of Court. The other two Inns of Court are Lincoln's Inn and Gray's Inn. These comprise the English University of Law. At one time students slept, ate and studied in these courts.

As you walk along, you will see the street that leads to **Lincoln's Inn** on your right where **Charles Dickens**

⑧ worked as an office boy at the age of 14. Now you will pass the **Royal Courts of Justice**, a magnificent building which houses the courts of appeal, probate, divorce, and others. If you detour into either of the courts of law on your right or left, you will be swept up in the world of the scholar and surrounded by winding walks, gardens, cul de sacs, sculpture and ancient, ivied buildings.

But don't delay: proceed down Fleet Street in the direction of **Covent Garden**, which is your goal this afternoon. As you walk along, you come to **Temple Bar,** a strange dragon-like memorial in the middle of the road, which marks the dividing line between The City of London and the City of Westminster. It is not very attractive, but at least it no longer displays the heads of executed prisoners, which used to be stuck on top as late as 1745.

⑨ Now past **St. Clement Danes**, the official church of the Royal Airforce Academy. Remember the old nursery rhyme, Oranges and lemons, say the bells of St. Clement's? Well, this is it. For any needle workers on this tour, take a quick look at the beautiful petit point hassocks hanging on hooks in each pew.

In the middle of the road, further on, you will come to
⑩ **St. Mary-le-Strand**, a Roman-looking church with beautiful blue windows. Go past the sweeping arc of Aldwych
⑪ on your right and **Somerset House** across the street on your left, occupied now by the Courtauld Institute Gallery, with its great Impressionist paintings; the Gilbert Collection of Decorative Art and the Hermitage Rooms with loans from the St. Petersburg Hermitage Museum.

Turn right on Wellington Street, which becomes Bow Street at Russell Street.

When you arrive at Russell Street, if you look a block
⑫ ahead you will see the **Royal Opera House;** a block to your right is the **Royal Theatre** (Drury Theatre). Turn left on Russell Street.

It will bring you to the area known as **Covent Garden.** In the Middle Ages, this was the convent garden of Westminster Abbey. By 1670, the Earl of Bedford had received a royal charter to hold forever a Market for fruits, flowers and vegetables. It remained London's main produce market until 1974, when it was moved to Nine Elms on the other side of the Thames across the Vauxhall Bridge. Nine Elms is covered by the largest stressed steel skin roof in Europe. It processes 4,000 tons of fruit and vegetables and 14,000 packages of flowers and plants daily.

Today's Covent Garden has been restored as a pedestrian shopping area and includes a wide variety of shops, bars and restaurants as well as the Jubilee Market, a crafts market adjacent to the garden.

Be sure to visit nearby **St. Paul's** church. The Earl of Bedford commissioned the great architect, Inigo Jones, to design a church for his property, but did not want to spend very much money: Not much better than a barn was his instruction. But Jones gave him the handsomest barn in England. Notice particularly the church portico; you will recognize the site where Henry Higgins finds Eliza Dolittle selling her violets in the musical, "My Fair Lady". Today you probably will find jugglers and fire eaters entertaining the crowd.

The rather odd little church garden can be entered from Henrietta Street or through the main gates on Bedford Street. Inside the church, look for the silver casket on the south wall bearing actress **Ellen Terry's** ashes. It is up a step or two, just to the right of the altar. This church is also the resting place for the famous carver, Grinling Gibbons.

DINNER

A S YOU WALK around the market place, begin to think about dinner and the special treat tonight at the

Ceremony of the Keys at the **Tower of London**. There are a number of places right in the central market, several within a block or two, but if you followed my advice at the beginning of this chapter, you have your reservations ⑬ at **Rules Restaurant** at 35 Maiden Lane. This fine eatery opened in 1798 and is one of London's oldest and most cherished restaurants. It is very British, slow and careful of service and a wonderful reward to yourself after a long day of sightseeing. They will take very good care of you.

After dinner, (if you wrote for your tickets to the **Ceremony of the Keys** at the Tower of London), you will cab to the main entrance of the Tower and arrive before 9:30 p.m. Allow about 20 minutes for this trip. For 700 years, the Chief Warder of the Tower has locked the gates at this hour and presented the keys to the Resident Governor. This is an ancient and moving ceremony, just one of the many beloved traditions still taking place in this remarkable city.

Get a good night's sleep. Tomorrow is another busy day and an early one.

DAY 2

Highlights: Westminster Abbey, the Houses of Parliament and Big Ben, Trafalgar Square, the National Portrait Gallery and Buckingham Palace.

Reservations: Plan to go to the theatre this evening. Check the theatre schedules in the daily newspapers or weekly magazines to select the performance you want to attend. See the Practical Information chapter for advice on getting tickets.

MORNING

① START THE DAY EARLY at **Westminster Abbey.** The tube stop is Westminster.

In early 1998, Westminster Abbey began charging

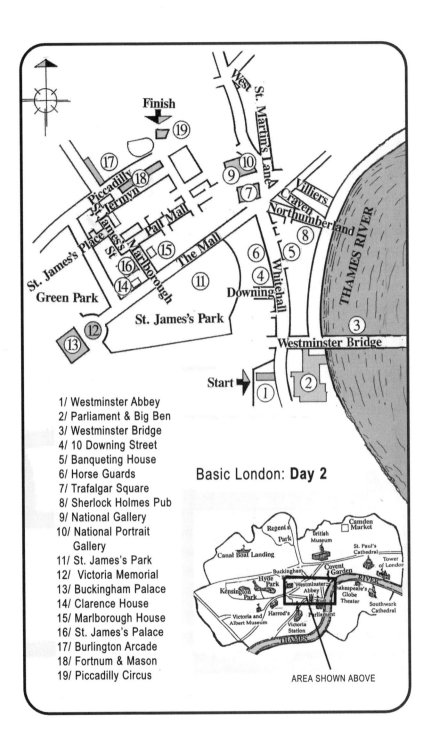

1/ Westminster Abbey
2/ Parliament & Big Ben
3/ Westminster Bridge
4/ 10 Downing Street
5/ Banqueting House
6/ Horse Guards
7/ Trafalgar Square
8/ Sherlock Holmes Pub
9/ National Gallery
10/ National Portrait Gallery
11/ St. James's Park
12/ Victoria Memorial
13/ Buckingham Palace
14/ Clarence House
15/ Marlborough House
16/ St. James's Palace
17/ Burlington Arcade
18/ Fortnum & Mason
19/ Piccadilly Circus

Basic London: **Day 2**

AREA SHOWN ABOVE

admission in an effort to control crowds. The entrance fee is about $12 for adults, lesser fees for students and seniors. Children under 11 are free. Family tickets for two adults and two children are available.

The Abbey is open Monday to Friday from 9 a.m. to 4:45 p.m., although please note, the last admission is at 3:45 p.m. Saturday 9 a.m. to 2:30 p.m. (last admission is 1:45 p.m.); on Sunday the Abbey is open only for services.

Another big change is that visitors will no longer enter through the west door of the nave but will use the **north entrance** into the north transept.

But take time to look at the installation of ten new life-size statues honoring Christian martyrs located above what used to be the Abbey's main entrance. The statues were unveiled in the summer of 1998 by the Archbishop of Canterbury, the Most Reverend George L. Carey, with Queen Elizabeth and the families of most of the martyrs in attendance.

The figures include Rev. Dr. Martin Luther King Jr., the American civil rights leader, assassinated in Memphis, Tennessee, in 1968, and Archbishop Oscar Romero, the liberal priest gunned down in El Salvador in 1980 while attending mass.

Others include the Polish priest Maksymilian Kolbe, who gave his life for another prisoner at Auschwitz in 1941; South African Manch Masemola, killed in 1928 by her animist parents for her Anglican faith; and Ugandan Anglican evangelist Janana Luwum, assassinated in 1976 by the Ugandan army.

Also memorialized are the Grand Dutchess Elizabeth of Russia, killed by the Bolsheviks; the German Lutheran theologian Dietrich Bonhoeffer, executed by the Nazis in 1945; Esther John, the Indian teacher and evangelist murdered at a mission in 1960; Lucian Tapiedi, evangelist of Papua New guinea, killed by a villager in 1942 when the

Japanese invaded; and Wang Zhimeng, a Chinese Christian executed in 1973 during the Cultural Revolution's drive against religion.

The limestone monuments tower 20 feet above visitors. They are intended to represent all those others who have died (and continue to die) in similar circumstances of oppression and persecution. They mark the end of a 25-year renovation of the abbey.

IF YOU TOOK THE TUBE TO THE ABBEY, you will arrive just opposite the **Houses of Parliament** and **Big Ben**. Take the pedestrian underpass toward Parliament and walk out onto **Westminster Bridge**. Look back at the famous view of Parliament. You can see up and down the Thames River.

If you have decided to cab to the abbey, take a few minutes after your tour to walk onto the bridge. As you leave the bridge and walk down Bridge Street, notice the statue of Winston Churchill directly ahead. On the other side of the grassy square is a statue of Abraham Lincoln.

Walk around the outside of **Parliament t**o admire this beautiful building, which is very often closed to visitors. Even if it is open, I do not recommend a tour on this quick tour of London. Do, however, notice the statues of Oliver Cromwell and Richard the Lion Heart on horseback, alongside the buildings. Cross over to visit the abbey; alongside, look up to see the gargoyles. If it is raining you will see their tongues acting as little waterspouts.

WESTMINSTER ABBEY was begun by Edward the Confessor in 1050; here William the Conqueror was crowned William II on Christmas Day in 1066, the first British coronation. Since then, every British monarch has been crowned here, and it has been the scene of many marriages and burials of British monarchs.

Enter the Abbey through the **North Door.** Just walk around for a few minutes and let feelings of wonder wash over you. Then walk down the main aisle toward the altar and at the sanctuary turn left: note the remarkable sculpture of Isaac Newton just inside the altar rail. Walk up the **North Ambulatory,** noting the **Queen Elizabeth** marble tomb in the same chapel with the small memorial containing the remains of bones found in the Tower, thought to be those of the little murdered princes. Read the label referring to Richard's perfidy.

SEE
WESTMIN-
STER
ABBEY
DETAIL
MAP

The **East Chapel is** dedicated to Royal Air Force fighters who fell in the Battle of Britain. Note the stained glass window which includes Shakespeare's lines, "We few, we happy few, we band of brothers" (Henry V).

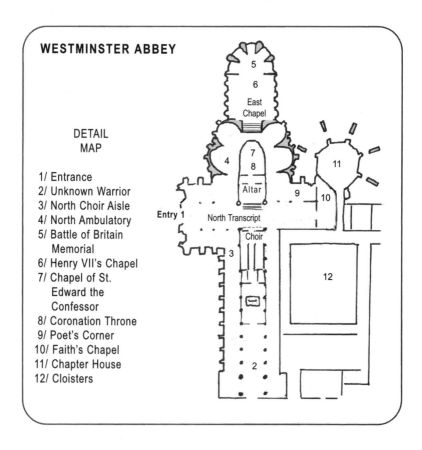

WESTMINSTER ABBEY

DETAIL
MAP

1/ Entrance
2/ Unknown Warrior
3/ North Choir Aisle
4/ North Ambulatory
5/ Battle of Britain
　　Memorial
6/ Henry VII's Chapel
7/ Chapel of St.
　　Edward the
　　Confessor
8/ Coronation Throne
9/ Poet's Corner
10/ Faith's Chapel
11/ Chapter House
12/ Cloisters

Oliver Cromwell's stone is directly in front of this chapel, indicating he was buried here from 1658-1661, only three years. He was then disinterred, and buried at Tyburn at Marble Arch. Later he, or at least his head, was buried in the Sydney Sussex Chapel in Cambridge.

W HEN YOU ENTER the jewel of the church, **Henry VII's Chapel**, your eyes automatically will go to the ceiling, the banners, the carvings and the statues. When you lower your eyes, you will find equally remarkable sights: the carvings on the choir stalls, great double gates, bronze panels and the tombs of Henry VII and Elizabeth of York.

Move on to the most sacred part of the abbey, the **Chapel of St. Edward the Confessor.** Cross a small bridge to enter; the chapel, in addition to Edward's marble shrine, contains the **Coronation Throne** on which every English monarch has been crowned. For coronations, the chair is moved to the high altar and covered with a cloth of gold. Below the seat is the **Stone of Scone**, of legendary and mythic importance.

As you leave St. Edward's Chapel *look carefully* for the entrance to the next chapel. Many people miss the doorway. This chapel includes the tombs of **Mary, Queen of Scots**, and Lady Margaret Beaufort, the mother of Henry VII. Some think hers is the finest tomb in Westminster. Notice the details such as the wrinkles in her statue's hands.

W ALK FURTHER ON and you arrive at the **Poet's Corner**. Here are buried or memorialized the most famous British writers, as well as an American, Henry Wadsworth Longfellow. Look for the fine Chaucer tomb, made of very dark marble almost hidden in the dark wall. The writings are so old they are almost illegible. Visit the not-so-fine memorial to Shakespeare; the strange bust of William Blake, and the memorials to such men of letters as Shelley, Milton, Browning, Byron, Dickens and Kipling.

I was in the abbey in 1973 for the dedication of the W. H. Auden stone. It was an extraordinary experience to see the laurel wreath laid on the stone, hear the boys' choir with their high soprano voices, listen to Stephen Spender and John Bjetleman, England's poet laureate, read Auden's words and extol him.

I happened to arrive at the abbey as this ceremony was beginning, one of those happy coincidences every traveler experiences somewhere along the way. Actor **Lord Laurence Olivier's** ashes were laid in the abbey in the spring of 1990. The memorial plaque can be found beside Irving and Garrick, beneath the bust of Shakespeare.

Faith Chapel, at the far end of Poet's Corner, is intended for private prayer and meditation. If you have a moment, enter and sit quietly, if only to admire its fine red and green frescoes.

Behind the abbey are the Chapter House, the Norman Undercroft, the Cloisters and the Abbey Museum. On this brief tour of the abbey, I will just recommend a quick visit to the **Chapter House**, built in 1250 and originally used for early meetings of Parliament, the cradle of all free parliaments.

As you enter, you will be asked to put on little cloth overshoes to protect the floor's red and gold tiles. Note particularly the wall paintings.

Take a minute to visit the Little Cloister with its fountain and flowerbeds.

Just one caveat: With all the new security measures, some places may be closed or restricted at certain times.

IF YOU DID NOT TUBE to the abbey, walk over to the **Westminster Bridge** for the lovely view of the **Houses of Parliament** and **Big Ben**.

Walk back to Parliament Street, which becomes

Whitehall, then past the Commonwealth offices and
Treasury on your left, to Downing Street, also on your left
but which is often blocked off for security reasons.
Number 10 Downing Street, the home of the Prime ④
Minister, is unassuming except for the guard and the
groups of tourists.

Back to Whitehall, with the Ministry of Defence on
your right and walk down to the **Horse Guards**. Stop to ⑤
admire the guards in their full-length capes, which almost
cover their knee-high polished black boots.

If you timed this right, you will arrive at 10:30 a.m.
(9:30 a.m. on Sunday) for the **changing of the guard.** I
like this much better than the one at Buckingham Palace,
primarily because the crowds are smaller and you can see
this one. People insist on petting the horses, which either
stand politely or snort at their visitors.

Across the street is the **Banqueting Hall**, built for just ⑥
what its name implies. The great building, designed by
architect Inigo Jones, is worth a quick stop to see the magnificent ceiling paintings by **Rubens.** Although this great
room was intended primarily for royal revelries, it was
from here that Charles I stepped through a window onto a
scaffolding for his beheading in 1649.

Proceed straight ahead on Whitehall with the Old
Admiralty on your left and Great Scotland Yard on your
right and you will debouch (a wonderful British word I
just love) into **Trafalgar Square.** It was built to memori- ⑦
alize Nelson's victory over the French and Spanish fleets
at Trafalgar in 1805.

Nelson's 185-foot column, topped with his 18-foot
likeness, overlooks the entire square. The four bronze
lions at the base were created by Sir Edwin Landseer. The
square is always filled with pigeons, tourists, and often
with political demonstrations.

Backing up the square is the **National Gallery of Art,**
and to your right, the church of **St. Martin in the Fields.**

NOON

B^Y NOW you are ready for lunch. Nearby Northumberland and Craven streets have numerous pubs and quick lunch places. The famous **Sherlock Holmes Pub** is located where Craven and Northumberland intersect. The **National Gallery** has a cafeteria with acceptable, inexpensive food.

AFTERNOON

G^O TO the **National Portrait Gallery,** located directly behind the National Gallery of Art. You can "do" this museum fairly rapidly for a quick look at British history. Every king, queen, artist, musician, writer, actor, prime minister and military person who was anybody in Britain is here; it is a collection of about 10,000 portraits, including photographs. Not all are on view at any given time.

Take the stairs or the elevator to the **second floor.** The collection is arranged chronologically, from the top floor to the bottom. Then walk down.

On the **mezzanine** are portraits from the Middle Ages. Room one is home to the Tudors: the wonderful Henry VIII cartoon, which was sketched for a fresco, and the portraits of Elizabeth I and Lady Jane Grey. Look for the famous Chandos portrait of Shakespeare, the first picture the gallery acquired.

Walk through the rooms at a steady pace just looking at what particularly interests you. **Room 13** has the only authentic portrait of Shelley, one of his wife Mary (the author of "Frankenstein", and a painting of his friend, Lord Byron, dressed in a Greek costume. **Room 15** contains Jane Austen's image, painted by her sister, Cassandra, and considered one of the gallery's treasures.

To reach the first floor and Room 16 walk down the back stairs. In Room 16 is the elegant painting of Queen

Victoria in her coronation regalia. **Room 17** has my favorite, the Bronte sisters painted by their brother, Branwell. It was found folded up; the creases still show. **Room 21** has Margaret Cameron's photographs of Carlyle and Tennyson, and Watts Choosing for which he used his wife-actress, Ellen Terry, as model.

All the royal portraits are on the **Main Floor** including those of **Princess Diana** and **Prince Charles**. The bookshop has black and white cards of every item in the collection as well as a large selection of other attractive gifts.

L ONDON is filled with lovely parks; no visit would be complete without a stroll through at least one of them. Walk back to Trafalgar, cross the square, walk under the Admiralty Arch and you will be on **The Mall.**

An entrance to **St. James's Park** is just opposite the ⑪ broad steps to Carlton House Terrace on your right and Horse Guards Road on your left. Walk to the lake with its ducks, geese and pelicans. The surprising pelicans are the offspring of a pair given to Charles II by the Russian Ambassador to England.

Walk along the lake to the first main path to your right, which will take you back to **The Mall.** Walk left ⑫ down the Mall to the **Victoria Memorial**, in front of ⑬ **Buckingham Palace.**

If the standard is flying atop the palace, the royal family is in residence. I suggest you walk back up the Mall to Marlborough Gate and St. James's Street on your left.

You will pass **Clarence House**, one of the royal resi- ⑭ dences.

As you turn left into Marlborough Street, **Marlborough House**, residence for important visitors, is ⑮ on your right and **St. James's Palace** on your left. None ⑯ of these buildings are open to the public on a regular basis, but you can walk into some of the courtyards. Jog a few steps to your left and then right on St. James's Street.

You will pass **Lobb's**, the bootery; **Lock & Co.**, for hats; and **Berry Bros.& Rudd** for wines; all in business since the 18th century. Do stop in one or more of them for a giant step into the past. Tiny little Pickering Place, next to Berry Bros., opens into a little square, which is said to be the site of the last duel fought in London.

Continue on St. James's Street to **Jermyn Street**. If you go one block further on you would come to Piccadilly with the Ritz Hotel just around the corner to your left.

I suggest Jermyn Street. Visit the royal perfumer **Floris;** the cheese-and-ham shop **Paxton and Whitehead;** and **Dunhill's** for pipes and tobacco.

(18)   At **Duke Street** you are at the back end of **Fortnum and Mason**, unlike any grocery you ever saw. The clerks are dressed in tails; ladies of the realm wander around buying caviar and quail's eggs. It is a good place to look and to ship home gifts of marmalade and shortbread.

You can also have tea here, or just a sweet, as the British say. Try the first floor bar or the mezzanine restaurant. Or, sit at the counter and have the best bitter chocolate soda in town.

Out the front door of Fortnum's and you are on
(17) **Piccadilly.** The **Burlington Arcade** is directly across the street, a glass-enclosed shopping mall. Walk up one side and back the other. Look for the beadle's (guards) in their fancy dress who have been here for a century.

Out on Piccadilly, and turn left, where you can walk to
(19) **Piccadilly Circus** and the statue of Eros, with hundreds of young people sitting at the base of the fountain, waiting for something or someone.

EVENING

Y OU ARE NOW in the center of the **theatre district.** If you took my advice you will have your tickets for the theatre this evening. Time for a quick supper, if your tea at Fortnum's was not sufficient, or on to the theatre. Remember most curtains in London are at 7:30 p.m.

A final reminder: if you want to eat after the theatre, restaurants usually do not take orders after 10:15 p.m.; the tubes stop running at midnight.

DAY 3

Highlights: British Museum, SoHo, Carnaby Street, Liberty's Department Store, Regent Park and the Queen's Garden, and Madame Tussaud's Waxworks.

MORNING

Y OU CAN START a little later this morning since the British Museum does not open until 10 a.m. On ①
Sunday it is open at 2:30 p.m. Take the tube to Tottenham Court Road or cab to the museum.

During the past few years, the British Library departed from the British Museum to its new premises near St. Pancras, liberating 40 percent of the museum site for a massive renovation project.

The museum's program of expansion and renewal was completed in the year 2003, which coincides with the 250th anniversary of the museum's founding.

This major renovation included the transformation of the great court and the reading room. Included were new bookshops, a terrace restaurant on the upper mezzanine floor, and a centre for education including two auditoria, a resource center and library.

Designed by Sir Norman Foster and Partners, the Great Court is open to all visitors from early morning until late evening.

Basic London: **Day 3**

Start

Russell
Museum

New Oxford

Soho Square

Carlisle

Charing Cross

Manette

Dean

Meard

Greek

Great Marlborough

Broadwick

Berwick

Ganton

Marshall

Carnaby

Peter

Finish

N

1/ British Museum

2/ Museum Travern

3/ Soho Square

4/ Liberty's

Regent's Park

Camden Market

British Museum

St. Paul's Cathedral

Canal Boat Landing

Tower of London

Buckingham Palace

Covent Garden

Hyde Park

Westminster Abbey

RIVER

Kensington Park

Shakespeare's Globe Theater

Southwark Cathedral

Victoria and Albert Museum

Harrod's

Parliament

Victoria Station

THAMES

Area shown in map

I suggest you spend from an hour-and-a-half to two hours in the museum, enough for you to see a small number of the most important objects in the collection. I think most people overload their minds when they go to a museum and end up remembering very little of what they have seen. It will be hard to walk through some galleries without stopping, but in the long run I suspect you will carry away happier memories if you are selective.

The great new **Reading Room** is directly in front of you, as if you could miss it; and the even newer **Enlightenment Gallery** is to your right in space once occupied by the British Library. It is filled with the results of scientific discoveries made over the past several hundred years. This huge gallery (300 feet long, 41 feet wide and 31 feet high) will take enormous amounts of time so I suggest an alternative. Turn to the left as you come in the front door. The **Great Egyptian Gallery** contains the famous **Rosetta Stone**, which was discovered in 1797 and provided the key to Egyptian hieroglyphs, a script previously unreadable. Note the huge statues of **Ramses II** and the giant **Scarab Beetle,** as if you could miss them. On your left are the Assyrian winged bulls.

Walk to the **Duveen Gallery**, which contains the **Elgin Marbles**, remarkable fragments of the Parthenon. The Greek frieze at eye level is a procession to Mt. Olympus. Either spend time in this gallery, reading labels and walking slowly around the room, or don't bother at all. Without spending some time here, it all looks like a bunch of rubbish. I suggest spending the time; it's well worth the effort.

Just to your left as you leave the Duveen Gallery, go to see the **Portland Vase**, a cameo glass from the 1st century B.C., with the top white layer carved away to reveal the lovely blue underneath. Look for the displays of the royal lion hunts from Nineveh. Zigzag left and right past the **Balawat Gates,** a reconstruction, and the postcard shop. You will be back in the Great Hall again.

Take the stairs to the second floor. Incidentally, you will find toilets on either side of the stairway.

Look for the **Egyptian Rooms** Numbers 61-66 with their mummies, mummy cases and other objects. Room 62 displays the splendid Egyptian burial masks. Do take time to visit little **Gallery 66**, with its Coptic portraits, one of my favorite places in the museum. Retrace your steps to the stairway and return to the main hall.

NOON

TIME FOR LUNCH. Just across the street from the British Museum on Museum Street is, you guessed it, the ② **Museum Tavern,** open at 11:30 a.m. This is one of my favorite pubs. The last time I was there I had the best shepherd's pie I ever ate, with fresh vegetables and some wonderful kind of pickle relish on the side. Get your food at the counter, your drink at the bar, and carry them to one of the tiny tables lining the walls.

AFTERNOON

AFTER LUNCH, walk up Museum Street to New Oxford Street. Turn right and go to Giles Circle where you will turn left into **Charing Cross Road**. This is the street of books. Walk down to Manette Street (Remember Dr. Manette from "The Tale of Two Cities" by Charles Dickens?). The great bookstore, **Foyles**, is here and you could spend the whole afternoon browsing.

Resist, if you can, and walk down Manette Street, under the arch of the Pillars of Hercules pub, turn right on ③ to Greek Street and in a block or so you will be at **Soho Square**. This area was originally the hunting fields outside the walls of what was then The City of London. Soho was the hunting call heard as foxes and rabbits were pursued across these grounds. During the 19th century, this was the worst slum area in London. Today, trendy Soho is the center for good food, drink, the movie industry, strip shows and other variations of the sex industry. It continues to be a hangout for artists, actors and craftspeople as well as the global village for people from around the world.

Soho Square was laid out in the 17th century. A poorly maintained statue of Charles II and a funny mock Tudor cottage in which gardeners can rest are in the center of the square. To your right, on Greek Street, is the **House of Barnabas,** built in 1750 and still a haven for homeless women.

WALK PART WAY around the square to Carlisle Street, take a short block to **Dean Street,** then turn left. Number 88 Dean Street is an 18th century shop; number 26 is where **Karl Marx** lived in a room above the present Italian restaurant; and number 49 is the old French Pub. Turn right on Meard Street to see some of Soho's earliest buildings. Jog left a few steps to Peter Street, which looks like an alley, but will take you to Berwick Street, where you will turn right to see the vegetable, fruit and flower markets, complete with sex shops.

Turn left on Broadwick Street with its noisy collection of shops. Jog right a few steps on Marshall Street and left on Ganton; you will arrive at Carnaby Street, once the home of the flower children's culture of the 60's. Look to your left on Carnaby to see what remains of those wild days. There are now a number of rather trend shops here.

Go right on Carnaby to Great Marlborough Street, where a left turn will bring you to Regent Street and the great department store, **Liberty's,** a Tudor-style building with a maze of shopping rooms. One whole floor contains fabrics including Liberty's silks. The Liberty scarves are a standard tourist purchase. Don't neglect the excellent bargain basement if you feel like shopping.

A note: Do not think you saw all of Soho. You just had a taste, and not even a look at the Chinese area on Gerrard street, the Italian and Greek shops and restaurants on Old Compton Street or Frith Street, where unemployed waiters gather, waiting to be hired.

Aᶠᵗᵉʳ ᵃˡˡ ᵗʰᵉ ⁿᵒⁱˢᵉ and hurly-burly of Soho, and shopping on Regent Street, take a cab or the tube to the tranquil area called **Regent Park.** Its original design was to link a park via Regent Street to the now-vanished Carlton House. It is a nice change for this busy afternoon.

Walk up Regent Street to Oxford Circus and take the tube to Bond Street on the Central Line; then change to the Jubilee Line to Baker Street. Notice the images of Sherlock Holmes on the walls of the Baker Street station.

If you are not inclined to take the tube, hail a cab and take it to the entrance of Regent's Park at York Bridge Road. A reminder: cabs are a good bargain in London.

If you haven't taken the tube, walk down **Marylebone Road,** past **London's Planetarium** and **Madame Tussaud's** remarkable waxworks. You will see St. Marylebone Church where **Elizabeth Barrett** and **Robert Browning** were married. Famous Wimpole Street is just beyond.

Turn left at York Gate and walk to the entrance of John Nash's park. The park is surrounded by magnificent buildings called terraces. It would be a day's trip to walk around the exterior of the park; today, just walk into the park but look to your right, left and ahead to glimpse those glistening terraces. On your left, look for the octagonal domes of Sussex Place and the exotic Mosque.

Walk past Regent's College on your left, across the Inner Circle, to **Queen Mary's Gardens.** If the roses are in bloom when you visit you will be in for a special treat.

A restaurant is on your left, near the boating lake; an open-air theatre is just ahead with a tearoom beyond it. If you walk to your right you will come to the **Broad Walk,** which will take you to the **London Zoo** with all its giant pandas from China and much, much more.

Whether you choose to walk in Queen Mary's Gardens, to explore the streams, flower beds and lake, or opt for a much longer trek to the zoo or around the perimeter of the park, you will sense the grandeur of the planning and construction of this magnificent part of London.

EVENING

IN THIS, your final evening, plan a **boat trip** to see illuminated London. During the summer months, boats from Westminster Pier go up and down the Thames River, often with a basket supper available.

These three days have given you a taste of this great city. I hope it will encourage you to come back again to sample more.

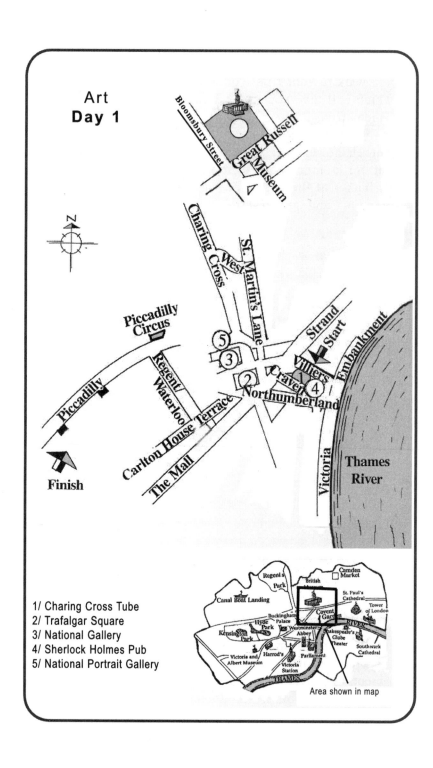

Art
Day 1

1/ Charing Cross Tube
2/ Trafalgar Square
3/ National Gallery
4/ Sherlock Holmes Pub
5/ National Portrait Gallery

ART LOVER'S
LONDON

What to see and most important
what to ignore (if you can)

LONDON IS THE HOME of more than 150 museums and galleries, ranging from great houses chock full of gorgeous paintings and furniture, to huge buildings filled with the treasures of the centuries.

Remember Britain was once the greatest empire in the world and, as great conquerors are wont to do, the British collected treasures from all over the world to bring home to their capitol, London. The Elgin Marbles, those wonderful friezes removed from the Parthenon in Greece and now in the British Museum, were not the only objects liberated by the British during years of empire building.

Many great British collections were developed by individuals with enormous wealth and impeccable taste. It is these fine individual collections which form the basis for most of the great museums in London.

IT WOULD BE IMPOSSIBLE to get more than a glimpse of some of these collections in three days, but let's have a go at it. I have chosen seven major museums to visit.

More importantly, I am going to suggest specific objects or rooms to view. I have learned that if I go to a museum and look at 400 objects, I cannot remember any of them; but if I go and have a good look at 12 objects, I may remember eight of them.

Once in the Pitti Palace in Florence, I left in tears when I realized I could not remember what I had seen in the gallery I had just visited. I had over-dosed on art.

Try it my way. I know it will be hard, often impossible, to walk through rooms of gorgeous things and not really look, but try it on this short visit and see if it works.

My selections are just that: my choices. If you have different and more specific interests such as German Expressionism, which is not one of my passions, do go to see them, but try my technique and look at only a few of the paintings.

Now for a couple of bookkeeping details. Museums in London are just like those at home except many are free. Do visit the museum shops. Most of them are first-rate and have gorgeous, inexpensive catalogues of their collections and special exhibitions.

You can check your coat and parcels in most museums, usually free of charge. Some places require checking of umbrellas and other objects. Special security these days may have other requirements, such as identification checks.

Works of art are loaned, reinstalled, and taken down for conservation. My suggestions for touring museums will help, but no tour can be totally accurate given the nature of a living organism such as a museum.

I suggest attending the theatre each of the three evenings in this tour I also recommend having supper following the performances. Since I cannot possibly know exactly where you will be attending a production, it is equally impossible to suggest a nearby restaurant. But here are a number of excellent suggestions for supper following the theatre. They all serve dinner till at least 11 p.m., some until midnight. But remember, the Tube stops running at midnight.

Do make reservations. There are a limited number of restaurants in London, which serve late in the evening, and they are always crowded. *Reserve.*

On or near St. Martin's Lane: **Salisbury Pub,** 90 St. Martin's Lane. Very chic and fun place with lots of stained glass, brass fittings and fashionable folks.

Near Covent Garden: **Rules,** 35 Maiden Lane. Telephone 020 7836-5314. Serves until midnight, Monday through Saturday. Oldest restaurant in London. British food. Excellent.

Cafe des Amis, 11 Hanover Place. Telephone 020 7379-3444. Across from the Royal Opera House. Walls covered with theatre posters and restaurant filled with theater crowd. Serves until 11:30 p.m., Monday through Saturday.

Joe Allen, 13 Exeter, south of Covent Garden. Telephone 020 7229 4050. Hangout for actors and artists. Good American food. Difficult to find; look for a tiny light over the door and a brass plaque. Basement restaurant.

Soho: **Quo Vadis,** 26-29 Dean. Telephone 020 7736 7593. Intriguing works on walls and tables filled with the art crowd. Karl Marx lived upstairs of this 60 year old restaurant.

Now, on to your exploration of Art Lover's London.

DAY 1

Highlights: The National Gallery, The National Portrait Gallery, and the British Museum. Today you will visit three important museums. I am starting the tour at Trafalgar Square and ending at the British Museum.

MORNING

① ② START THE DAY at **Trafalgar Square. Charing Cross** is the closest tube stop. At the north end of the square, facing Lord Nelson's monument, the fountains and the pigeons, is a huge building, the **National Gallery.** It began in 1824, when Parliament purchased 38 paintings from the collection of John Julius Angerstein, a City banker, and has been expanded five times since then.

The National Gallery is open daily 10 a.m. to 6 p.m., Wednesday to 9 p.m. Free admission. 020 7747-2885.

AS YOU WALK PAST THE ELEGANT COLUMNS and up the stairway, note the mosaic floor with images of famous people representing ideas: Churchill as *Defiance* and Margot Fonteyn as *Delectation*, for example.

The Sainsbury Wing with paintings from 1260-1510 was designed by Venturi, Scott Brown of Philadelphia. It includes work by van Eyck, Piero, Botticelli, Bellini and Raphael.

I can only suggest visits to specific galleries which contain some of my favorite art works.

Room 53 displays The Wilton Diptych, for many years at Wilton House. It shows Richard II being presented to the Virgin and Child. The origin and purpose of these paintings are unknown, but the panels are exquisite.

The wonderful Dutch paintings are in galleries 16 to 18; Rembrandt's and Hals' in galleries 26 and 27. Room 28 is still my favorite room of Dutch paintings.

Hogarth's six satiric paintings, *The Marriage Contract,* are now next to Gainsborough's *Mrs. Siddons* and my favorite, *Mr. and Mrs. Andrews.*

The Turners are now in Gallery 34 including the famous *The Fighting Temerarie.* It shows the warship *Temerarie,* named for a French ship which fought at Trafalgar, being towed to its last berth by a modern steam tug. This painting is about age and youth as well as about the coming Industrial age. It is a remarkable and moving painting.

The Spanish paintings are now divided, with Velazquez, Murillo and Zurbaran in Gallery 29 and Goya in 39. The Impressionists with Van Gogh, Cezanne, Seurat, and Picasso are in Rooms 43 - 46.

You are now back in the main entry near the shop. I recommend the shop with its excellent and inexpensive postcards, catalogues and art books.

WALK NORTH on Charing Cross Road to visit the **National Portrait Gallery.** Admission is free ⑤ except for special exhibitions. It is open Monday to Wednesday, 10 a.m. to 6 p.m.; Thursday and Friday, 10 a.m. to 9 p.m.; Saturday and Sunday, 10 a.m. to 6 p.m. For additional information call the information line 020 7312 2463.

The National Portrait Gallery has paintings of everyone who was important in English history: statesmen, generals, kings and queens, artists, actors, scientists, writers in a word, everyone.

Start on the **top floor**, which you can reach by lift (elevator) or stairs. Just work your way down, pausing by the portraits of people you find most interesting. This is a smaller, very manageable museum and one of my very favorites in London. You can "do" it in an hour and a half unless you become totally fascinated by the images.

NOON

THE GALLERY has a café and an excellent bookstore. If you would like to try a pub lunch, walk across Trafalgar Square and down Northumberland Avenue to the ④ **Sherlock Holmes Pub**. This is an extremely popular spot; in nice weather you will find lots of customers standing in the street. A re-creation of Holmes' Baker Street study is on the first floor next to the pub and there are memorabilia of the fictional detective throughout the building.

The fine Greek restaurant, **Beoty's**, is on St. Martin's Lane, across from the National Gallery.

AFTERNOON

⑤ On to the **British Museum.** You can walk the ten blocks north on Charing Cross Road to Great Russell Street, turn right for about three blocks/or take a short cab ride/or take the tube from Charing Cross to Totttenham.

If you choose to walk on Great Russell Street, look for I. Cornelissen & Son at number 105. This shop has been providing art supplies since 1855. You can find everything from quills to gold leaf, plus a real feeling of history. Pleasant, helpful people.

On to the gorgeous newly remodeled British Museum. The main entrance is on **Great Russell Street**, but you can also enter on Montague Street. The museum is open from 10 a.m. to 5:30 p.m. Galleries are often closed during certain hours. Check open gallery hours at the visitor's desk.

The British Museum (or BM as the Brits call it...don't you love it?) was founded in 1753 and housed at Montague House, the site of the present museum. The great British Library which was once housed here is now located in a new museum near St. Pancras railway station.

As part of Britain's nod to the millenium, Architect Sir Norman Foster designed the new entrance, courtyard, and

Reading Room. At a cost of a hundred-and-fifty-million dollars, the British got their money's worth. It is stunning. Facing the visitor is the great round **Reading Room,** graceful staircases and a glass and steel dome with a veil of latticework.

Stone stairs wind around the "drum" and lead to a **restaurant.** Hours are approximately the same as the open hours for the museum. They provide morning coffee, afternoon tea and evening dinners, plus an all day menu of hot and cold meals. If you want to make a reservation call 020 7323 8990.

WHERE DO YOU START? With its two-and-a-half miles of galleries this can be a daunting decision. I am going to suggest a possible itinerary, but if you get waylaid by your special interest in Greek, Roman, Egyptian or Chinese artifacts, just stop and enjoy.

In the spring of 2004, the museum opened their **Enlightenment Gallery** in the space formerly occupied by the British Library...a Greek Revival hall, 300 feet long, 41 feet wide and 31 feet high. It is filled with objects inspired by the results and explorations of eighteenth century scientists..covering nature, archaeology, antiquity and primitive people. This includes 16,000 eighteenth century and early nineteenth century books on loan from the House of Commons Library.

The Enlightenment Gallery is to your right as you enter the Great Court. To your left you will find the stairs (and elevators) leading to the Egyptian, Greek Roman and Asian galleries. Incidentally, the British Museum web site has very handsome floor plans...in color..with helpfully numbered galleries. www.thebritishmuseum.ac.uk/visit/maps.

The great **Egyptian gallery** (number 4) contains the *Rosetta Stone* which was discovered in 1797 and provided the key to Egyptian hieroglyphs, a scrip previously unreadable. Note the huge statues of Rameses II and the giant scarab beetle.

Continue to **Gallery 18** which contains the *Elgin Marbles*. In 1803 Lord Elgin rescued the fragments of the Parthenon which remained after an explosion in 1687. The frieze, which is at eye level, consists of human figures and horses in procession to Mt. Olympus. Either spend time in this gallery reading labels and really looking or don't bother at all. I recommend spending the time. Take the stairs to the second floor. **Galleries 61 to 66** contain the incredible collection of Egyptian artifacts, including mummies, mummy cases, and portrait and burial masks. Circle around through galleries **50 to 59** with their Mesopotamia treasures. And look for galleries **40 to 45** to view objects from the *Sutton Hoo Ship-Burial,* relics of an East Anglican chief of about 625 A.D., discovered in 1939, and the Mildenhall Treasure, the greatest treasure of Roman silver ever found in the British Isles, discovered in 1946 by Gordon Butcher, a Suffolk ploughman. Incidentally, if you want to know more about Gordon Butcher's great discovery, go to the museum's shop and look for Roald Dahl's wonderful book. Remember Dahl's book, *James and the Giant Peach*? Well, it is the same author, but a different and amazing new story about some very old objects.

I THINK NOW is about time for some other kind of sustenance. As I noted earlier, the museum has lovely new restaurants up the stairs, behind the Reading Room.

Or if you want something quite different and equally wonderful, walk out the front doors, down the great staircase, across Great Russell Street to the 1703 Museum Pub...I think they call it the **Museum Tavern** now..but it is still filled with the most incredible oak paneling, cut glass and velvet seats you could ever want. It serves great traditional English food such as shepherd's pie. Get your ale at the bar; food at a counter in the back and try to relax in this very busy extraordinary place.

EVENING

TIME FOR A REST and food again. If you plan to go to the theatre this evening, I recommend a good tea if you didn't take advantage of the **Museum Pub,** since you will not have time for a leisurely dinner before curtain time. Remember: most curtains are at 7:30 p.m.; you can always have supper after the theatre.

Since so many restaurants do not serve late in the evening, remember, the rush on those that do is tremendous. Check the recommendations at the beginning of this chapter.

DAY 2

Highlights: The Wallace Collection and the Victoria and Albert Museum.

Reservations: Supper reservations: Daquise, 20 Thurloe St., 020-7589 6117 or La Bouchee, 56 Old Brompton Road, 020-7589 1929.

MORNING

THE WALLACE COLLECTION on Manchester Square, is open Monday through Saturday from 10 a.m. to 5 p.m., Sunday from noon to 5 p.m. Admission is free. The closest Tube station is Bond Street on the Central Line. Walk north on Duke Street (which becomes Mandeville Place) to Manchester Square # 7 to reach the Wallace Collection on the north side of the square.

The bulk of the collection was formed by the 4th Marquess of Hertford, inherited by his son, Sir Richard Wallace, who brought it from Paris to England. Lady Wallace gave the collection to the nation on the condition

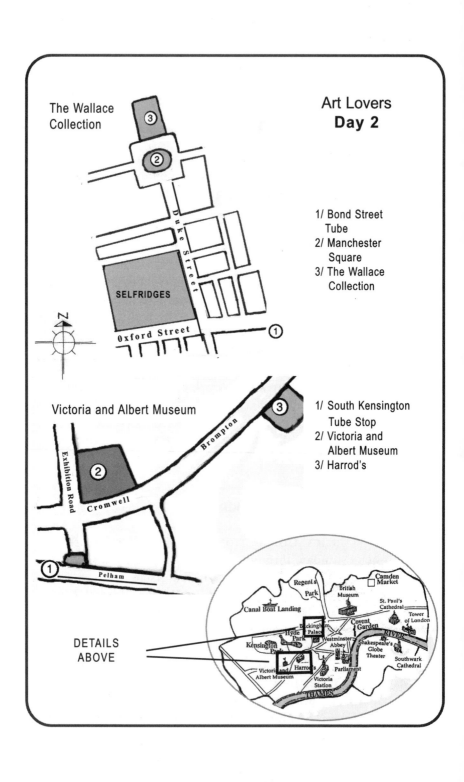

The Wallace
Collection

Art Lovers
Day 2

1/ Bond Street
   Tube
2/ Manchester
   Square
3/ The Wallace
   Collection

SELFRIDGES

Duke Street

Oxford Street

N

Victoria and Albert Museum

1/ South Kensington
   Tube Stop
2/ Victoria and
   Albert Museum
3/ Harrod's

Exhibition Road

Brompton

Cromwell

Pelham

DETAILS
ABOVE

Regent's
Park

British
Museum

Camden
Market

St. Paul's
Cathedral

Tower
of London

Canal Boat Landing

Covent
Garden

Buckingham
Palace

Hyde
Park

Westminster
Abbey

Shakespeare's
Globe
Theater

RIVER

Kensington
Park

Southwark
Cathedral

Victoria and
Albert Museum

Harrod's

Parliament

Victoria
Station

THAMES

that nothing be added to or removed from it. The public was first admitted in 1900. Here you will visit a grand house with its paintings, furniture, draperies, rugs and art objects in place; only the family is missing.

During the Millenium year of 2000, the National Lottery provided almost $16 million to overhaul the building housing the Wallace Collection. American architect, Rich Mather, designed a gorgeous glass roof to cover the new central courtyard. This "winter-garden" is home to the Café Bagatelle, open during museum hours. Beneath it are education rooms, a library and lecture hall and temporary exhibition space.

The galleries have also undergone some remarkable changes: replacing the original rich fabrics on the walls, hanging heavy silk curtains and enriching the already remarkable collections.

Remember, the British ground floor is the same as our first floor and their first floor is our second floor and so on. I still get confused by this. Just walk leisurely through the rooms on the ground floor, looking at all the magnificent objects.

The book and card shops are to your left as you enter; the sculpture garden and Café directly in front of you.

Just in back of the shop is **Room 12** filled with English and French paintings of the 1820s and 30s. I mention this room in particular because it contains paintings by Richard Bonnington, the remarkable English painter. I "discovered" him in this room years ago and still like to "visit" his landscapes, portraits and seascapes and to remember that he lived a very short 26 years, 1802 – 1828..the result of "consumption", now called tuberculosis.

Also look for the painting of *Edward V and the Duke of York* (the little princes) in the Tower by the French painter Delaroche.

Rooms 8 - 11 are filled with an extraordinary collection of European armor. Look for the Sevres porcelain and the cabinet work by the French masters Boulle, Cressent and Riesener.

In **Room 3** notice the magnificent chandelier and the roll top desk, a copy of one now in Versailles.

Circle back to the Entrance Hall and walk up the white marble staircase to the **first floor** with the most popular galleries. Notice the Boucher paintings on the stairway as well as the wrought iron and bronze balustrade you are gripping and the bright red carpet.

In **Room 13** Guardi and Canaletto paintings vie for attention; Rooms 18 - 20 have the Rubens oil sketches for tapestries.

Room 22 is the largest room and holds the most famous paintings in the collection: Rembrandt's painting of his son *Titus*; Hals' *Laughing Cavalier,* perhaps the best known painting in this collection; Velasquez's *Lady with a Fan*; and great paintings by Reynolds and Gainsborough. Gainsborough's painting of *Mrs. Robinson (Perdita)* hangs next to Lawrence's painting of *George IV*.

Room 24 is filled with some of the best French 18th century paintings in the collection as well as gorgeous furniture. Again Fragonard and Boucher as well as Watteau and Lancret fill the room with their romantic and beautiful paintings. I especially like Fragonard's *The Swing*.

Be sure to notice the fabulous furniture, including some made for Marie Antoinette.

Do lift the covers off cases in the center of the room to look at the miniatures. You can spend hours in this extraordinary house with its incredible collections.

NOON

THIS MIGHT BE a good time to visit the **Café Bagatelle** for lunch.

AFTERNOON

THERE ARE SEVERAL WAYS to reach the **Victoria and Albert Museum** from the Wallace: return to the Bond Street Tube stop, take the Jubilee line one stop to Green Park and transfer to the Picadilly line to the South Kensington Stop. The V and A is a short two block walk north to Cromwell North.

Or walk a block west of the Wallace Collection to Baker Road and take Bus 74 which will eventually deposit you in front of the V and A. Just remember the traffic flows in the opposite direction from American routes, so be sure you are going south.

Or you can take the easy but a bit more expensive route and just put up your hand to hail one of London's famous black cabs.

The cab will deposit you in front of the Exhibition Road entrance. The V & A is open, free of charge, from 10 a.m. to 5:45 p.m., daily; Wednesdays until 10 p.m.

The **New Restaurant** serves meals or just coffee, tea and cakes from Monday through Sunday, 10 a.m. to 5:30 p.m. Late view candlelit dinners are served on Wednesdays from 7 to 10 p.m. On Sundays, from 11 a.m. to 3 p.m., you can eat brunch and listen to some of the best jazz in town for about $15. Price guaranteed to change.

The museum is constantly renovating displays, which can involve closing galleries for months, and warns in its information brochure that galleries are sometimes closed without notice owing to shortage of staff. It is important to remember all of these admonitions so that you will not be too disappointed if you cannot see all the galleries I recommend.

Enter the museum at **Exhibition Road** entrance. Walk through the entrance hall, Room 49: the shop will be to your left.

This is the Index Corridor. Directly ahead of you is the Medieval Treasury room. On your right are the art of China gallery and the Japanese Gallery.

Exit at the far end of the Japanese Gallery into Galleries 22, 23 and 24 with their collections of Gothic Art from Italy, England, France and Germany.

In **Gallery 25,** to your right, visit the large altar piece with scenes from the life of St. George.

Continue along **Galleries 26 and 27** to see art from the Northern European Renaissance. Cut through Gallery 29 to **Gallery 38** to see the Medieval Tapestries.

Circle around the garden, which is to your left, to **Galleries 16 and 15,** Italian Renaissance. In fact, do not circle around these gardens. Take the time to visit them, especially if it is a hot summer day...you will find no place pleasanter. And take a moment to look at two ceramic plaques on the south side which are in memory of Sir Henry Cole's dogs. It is also a reminder that it was Cole who created this museum...first as the South Kensington Museum and later as the V&A in 1899.

Just beyond Galleries 16, 15 and 14 are three extraordinary rooms: the **Poynter Room** or Dutch kitchen, with its Minton blue and white tiles and stained glass window; the **Gamble Room,** with its decorated ceiling and columns; and the **Morris Room** or Green Dining Room, with its Burne-Jones panels.

Follow the Italian Renaissance from Rooms 13 to 20. Turn right into **Room 21** with objects from the High Renaissance 1500-1600.

THIS WOULD BE A GOOD TIME to stop for something to eat or drink. Walk through Room 21 to the entry way off Exhibition Road, turn right and walk through the Rodin sculpture to the steps which will take you downstairs to the **Henry Cole Wing** and the **restaurant.**

The wing with its seven floors is filled with paintings,

prints, miniatures and watercolors.

And I am only taking you to the restaurant. If you insist, you might want to see the huge collection of Constable paintings, watercolors and drawings on the sixth level of this building. The restaurant is extremely handsome and the food is admirable and inexpensive.

R ETRACE YOUR STEPS UPSTAIRS and back through Gallery 21. Turn to your right to see the famous dress collection in **Gallery 40.** The museum staff tells me that 25 percent of visitors come to see this collection of costumes, which range from the 16th to 20th century.

Walk across the hallway to **Gallery 48** to see the enormous room containing the astounding Raphael Cartoons. The museum has 7 of the 10 Raphael designs for tapestries woven in Brussels for the Sistine Chapel in Rome.

Cross back to **Gallery 47,** filled with Indian sculpture including Tipu's Tiger, a large wooden model of a tiger mauling a British officer. Inside is a small organ which reproduces the groans of the unfortunate victim, but that is not operational now, so it is not as gruesome as it sounds.

Gallery 41 is filled with Indian Art, including the fine Mughal rugs.

The Art of Islam in **Gallery 42** will bring you full circle and back to the entrance and shop

If you have either the time or interest, walk the length of Corridor 47 to the **Victorian and Italian cast courts,** which opened in 1873. As you can tell from the name, these enormous skylit rooms are filled with copies of works of art. This kind of copying was very popular at the time for study purposes but fell out of favor in the 20th century when foreign travel became more affordable. Only recently has there been a revived interest in the collection because of its quality.

I have to admit I love these galleries and was totally

astonished the first time I walked into one to see the exact copy of Trajan's enormous column sitting in the middle of the room.

As you walk around these two rooms, you will see copies of many of the world's greatest sculptures, from Michelangelo's *David* and *Moses* to the 12th century *Portico de La Gloria* from Santiago de Compostela. However you may feel about copying works of art, I think you will be amazed at this collection and the architectural courts in which they are displayed.

I was amused to find a cast of a large fig leaf hanging behind the copy of the David statue. A sign read it was hung on the cast on the occasion of visits by royal ladies. The fig leaf was originally used on the visit of Queen Victoria, and last used for the late Queen Mary when she was Queen Mother.

And finally a visit to the **top floor** to take a look at a suite of five renovated painting galleries, originally built in the 1850's. They are part of the V and A's 10-year plan to present its collections in new ways. **Room 88 a** is filled with watercolors and drawings; **Room 88** with Gainsborough and Constable oil sketches; **Room 87** with Constable and Turner landscapes, **Room 82** with John Sheepshank's collection of paintings and drawings and **Room 81** with the collection of Constantine Alexander Ionides, including 80 paintings by Renaissance, pre-Raphaelite and French painters. It is totally possible that by the time you read this, some of these exhibitions will have changed, but whatever is in these rooms and the rooms "to come" will be worth a visit.

Be sure to visit the **museum shop**. It has a fine assortment of material about the museum's collection and other art-related books and objects. At the side is a small alcove containing articles, especially fine glass work, made by British craftspeople.

Your visit has enabled you to see the art of the major

civilizations, the art of the Renaissance including the tap-
estry collection, the great dress collection and several of
the museum's fine period rooms.

On future visits you can go upstairs to see the jumble
of British furniture and painting, the incredible ironwork,
bronzes, jewelry, armor, embroidery, enamels, silver and
musical instruments.

There seems to be no end to this museum, but you
have made a start.

EVENING

SINCE THIS HAS BEEN a long and probably tiring day, I
am going to suggest having a pleasant, quiet meal
instead of racing to the theater. And there are a couple of
very nice places just south of the V & A museum.

I am enamored of a small French restaurant at 56
Brompton Road, **La Bouchee.** It is small so do, I repeat,
do make a reservation (020-7589-1929). It has a menu, but
also a chalk board with the day's specials...check the specials. I still remember a coq au vin that made me whim-
per...and I am not much of a whimperer.

The second place is **Daquise,** 20 Thurloe St., near the
South Kensington station. You probably don't need a
reservation, but just in case, the number is 020 7589 6117.
It is Polish and a bit loud sometimes and maybe a bit
dowdy, but the food is very good and maybe after all the
correct and perfect places you have been today, it might
offer a welcome change. Just a thought.

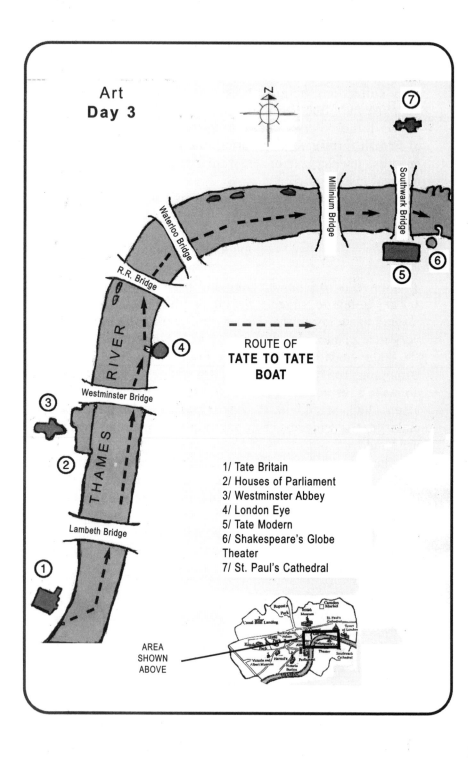

Art
Day 3

N

Waterloo Bridge

Millinium Bridge

Southwark Bridge

R.R. Bridge

RIVER

⑦

⑥

⑤

④

Westminster Bridge

THAMES

③

②

Lambeth Bridge

①

ROUTE OF
**TATE TO TATE
BOAT**

1/ Tate Britain
2/ Houses of Parliament
3/ Westminster Abbey
4/ London Eye
5/ Tate Modern
6/ Shakespeare's Globe
Theater
7/ St. Paul's Cathedral

AREA
SHOWN
ABOVE

DAY 3

Highlights: Tate Britain, London Eye (Ferris wheel) and Tate Modern

Reservations: Lunch at Tate Britain restaurant: Phone 020 7887 8825 or Tate Modern on level 7: Phone 0207 401 5020.

Reservations to ride the London Eye (Ferris Wheel): Phone 0870 5000 600 (8:30 a.m. to 8 p.m.) for same day booking. Or book on line (www.ba-londoneye.com/booking). Must be made 14 hours in advance.

Tickets will be waiting for you on arrival, but plan to be at the site at least one-half hour in advance of booking for the 35 minute trip. The "Eye" is open daily from 10 a.m. to 7 p.m. (8 p.m. April to May and mid September to the end of September.)

MORNING

S TART THE DAY at **Tate Britain** which houses works of art by British artists from the fifteenth century to the present. The **Tate Modern**, which you will visit this afternoon, exhibits twentieth-century British art formerly displayed here. In 2001, Tate Britain opened ten new and five refurbished galleries as well as a new entrance off of Atterbury Street.

Tate Britain has been able to revert to Henry Tate's original vision of a national gallery of British art. The museum is located on the north bank of the River Thames at Millbank, southwest of London center and south of the Houses of Parliament. The closest underground station is Pimlico. A number of buses service this area including the 77A which goes past Trafalgar Square, south of Whitehall along Millbank. A cab may be the preferable choice.

The galleries are open, with free admission, daily from 10 a.m. to 5:30 p.m. There are four entrances: the new Manton Entrance on Atterbury Street, the traditional entrance on Millbank, the Clore gallery entrance to the right of the main Millbank entrance and the North entrance on John Islip Street at the back of the gallery which has ramp access and parking for disabled visitors.

The **Clore Gallery**, designed by architect James Stirling, houses J.M.W. Turner's bequest of his works to the nation. The handsomely lit and designed galleries compliment the glowing sea paintings by Turner.

The museum now contains ten new and five refurbished galleries, a new information center and a total regrouping of works of art. The collection has been regrouped into rooms around specific themes, some focusing on particular artists. A new suite of rooms displays new acquisitions.

My best advice at this point in the museum's history is to get a new map at the information center since changes are being continuously made. Generally, the earliest art is in the western half of the gallery near the Manton entrance and the most recent work, since 1900, in the eastern half of the museum.

The highlights in the museum are the Turner paintings, the William Blake, Hogarth, Gainsborough and Reynold paintings and the pre-Raphaelites, including Burne-Jones and John Millais.

If you made a luncheon reservation here, look for the **Rex Whistler** room with its stunning murals on four walls. This is an extraordinarily good restaurant with some of the best and lowest-priced wines in London. The restaurant is open daily for lunch, noon to 3 p.m., Monday through Saturday and Sundays until 4 p.m.

The only reason I could suggest seeing the "Two Tates" and the "London Eye" on the same day is because of the "new" Thames boat service. The **"Tate to Tate"**

boats run every forty minutes during gallery opening hours between the Tate Modern and Tate Britain. The boat also stops at the London Eye. Tickets are available from both museums and are valid for use all day...you may make as many trips as you wish. An adult ticket costs about $10.

A **new pier**, located in front of Tate Britain at Millbank, was designed by David Marks and Julia Barfield, designers of the London Eye. The boat is a state-of-the-art 220 seat catamaran.

IF YOU DECIDE to take a ride on the **London Eye** (Ferris wheel), give yourself at least one hour and one half, then take the "Tate to Tate" boat to the **Bankside pier** in front of the Tate Modern.   ④

The first designs for The Eye were made by the husband and wife team Marks and Barfield in 1993 on their kitchen table in South London. They had entered a competition to design a millenium landmark; the contest was scrapped. They never gave up and eventually interested British Airways in the project.

It became the largest observation wheel ever built. Over 1,700 people in five countries would be involved in building it. Transportation of the component parts had to be timed to co-ordinate with tides in the Thames River, so that the large sections could safely negotiate London's bridges. The 32 passenger capsules had to be designed to be within the maximum width allowed on the French roads over which they made their way to the English Channel and up the Thames...just to give you an idea of the complexity of building this 450 foot-high-wheel with its 32 air-conditioned capsules.

The 30-minute rotation enables you to see about 25 miles on a clear day...assuming you happen to have a "clear" day in London.

This is one of the most popular attractions currently in

London, so do give yourself enough time and order tickets in advance as I have suggested.

⑤ THEN BACK to the wonderful **Tate to Tate boat** to continue your trip to the **Tate Modern,** located on the
south bank of the river Thames, almost opposite **St.**
⑦ **Paul's Cathedral.**

The museum is located in the original Bankside Power Station, redesigned by Swiss architects Herzog and de Meuron. It features a 325 foot central chimney and a glass canopy extending the length of the roof, plus a gorgeous café featuring not only great food but outstanding views of London.

The Tate Modern is open Friday to Thursday, 10 a.m. to 7:30 p.m.; Friday and Saturday 10 a.m. to 10 p.m. Admission is free but like most of the "free" museum in London, they are happy to accept donations.

There are two entrances: one is on the north side, on either side of the chimney and is accessed from the river walkways. The West Entrance is on Holland Street, via a ramp, extending down into the main hall: The Turbine Hall and Level 1.

There are two restaurants: the **Restaurant** on the top, level 7. As noted earlier, make reservations...they take no reservations for lunch on Saturday or Sunday. The **Tate Modern Café** is on level 2 and overlooks gardens. Open 10 a.m. to 6 p.m. Sunday to Thursday; 10 a.m. to 10 p.m. Friday and Saturday. There is also an **espresso bar** on level 4 with balconies, open daily 10 a.m. to 6 p.m.

It is impossible to give a step-by-step tour of this amazing space since exhibitions and installations are changed so often. There is a ten-minute audio tour of the building available in Turbine Hall.

You can be sure of seeing some of Henri Matisse's great paper cut-outs, works by Francis Bacon, Monet, Magritte, Giacometti and German expressionists as well as temporary installations of enormous sculptures by modern artists. **Level 4** usually has major loan exhibitions.

W HEN YOU LEAVE the museum, walk down to the river. There you will see Sir Norman Foster's famous **Millennium Bridge** connecting this south bank to the ⑥ north bank near **St. Paul's Cathedral**. After some initial ⑦ difficulties inherent in suspension bridges, it is very solid now.

Next door to the Tate Modern is **Shakespeare's Globe** ⑧ **Theater.** There are performances from May to September. Call the box office for tickets: 020/7401-9919.

The Royal National Theater is north of the Tate Modern. You can see the classics as well as contemporary works at one of its three theaters. Check theater listings for current productions. There are bars, cafes, performances, and terraces here for the visitor.

A S YOU CAN SEE, there are many choices of how to spend your last evening in the great theatrical London.

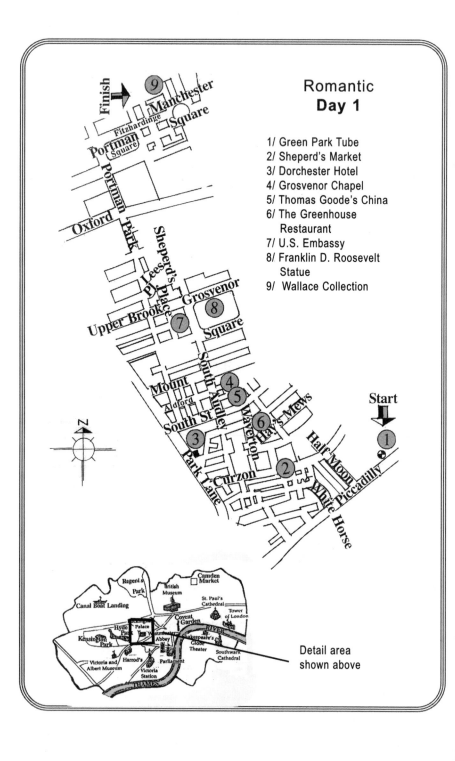

Romantic
Day 1

1/ Green Park Tube
2/ Sheperd's Market
3/ Dorchester Hotel
4/ Grosvenor Chapel
5/ Thomas Goode's China
6/ The Greenhouse
  Restaurant
7/ U.S. Embassy
8/ Franklin D. Roosevelt
  Statue
9/ Wallace Collection

Finish

Start

Detail area
shown above

ROMANTIC
LONDON

No city has more for travelers
with romance in their souls

WHEN YOU THINK OF ROMANTIC CITIES you may think first of Paris, Venice or Vienna, but probably not London. What makes a city romantic? Gardens, parks, pretty restaurants, lakes and rivers, strolling paths, flowers, music and art. London has them all.

Consider this:

Your three-days in London will include a leisurely walk through the most elegant part of this fabulous city, a boat trip following the path of kings and queens, a night cruise to see illuminated London, a picnic in an elegant park, rooftop dining and an outdoor theatre performance in the Queen's rose garden.

Your days will start later in the mornings, be more unhurried and not so filled with sightseeing as some of the other tours all befitting your Romantic London.

DAY 1

Highlights: Mayfair, Shepherd's Market, Grosvenor Chapel and Square, the Wallace Collection and the Dorchester Hotel.

Reservations: Lunch reservations at The Greenhouse, 27a Hays Mews. Telephone 020-7499 5368.

Evening: Open air theatre in Regent's Park. Check newspapers or magazines to see whether there is a production and time of performance. Call to reserve tickets.

WHAT BETTER PLACE to start than in the most elegant part of London: Mayfair with its Rolls Royces; men with bowler hats and tightly furled umbrellas; ladies, hatted and gloved and sipping tea; and rows of town houses and antique shops.

The original May Fair, from which this part of London takes its name, was held in Shepherd's Market two weeks each year from late 1680 to the mid-1700's. This is the area which satirists Trollope and Thackeray wrote about in their novels of power and wealth and in which Evelyn Waugh's *Brideshead Revisited* was set. Shepherd's Market is now filled with small houses, shops, cafes, a little marketplace and the famous pub, Shepherd's.

MORNING

① START THE DAY in **Sheperd's Market** about 10 a.m. The **Green Park tube** stop is closest or cab to the market. If you take the tube, walk west on Piccadilly to either White Horse Street or Half Moon Street.

② If you turn right on either one of them, you will arrive at the center of **Sheperd's Market.** You will remember Half Moon Street is where P.G. Wodehouses's Jeeves took such good care of Bertie Wooster.

The market area stretches to your left and is filled with lovely shops, restaurants, pubs and interesting buildings. Explore the whole area, walking up and down the little mews, stopping for a cup of coffee or tea and a scone at one of the cafes.

After your exploration in the market, walk up to Curzon Street. Trumpers, the royal barbershop is at number 10. Take a look in the window.

Walk west on Curzon Street to Park Lane, turn right
and walk up past the fancy **Dorchester Hotel** until you ③
come to Aldford Street. Turn right to see the Victorian
houses and the lovely **Grosvenor Chapel** directly ahead. ④
The chapel was built in 1730 and was adopted by the
American forces in 1939-45.

When you come to South Audley, turn right for a block
to see **Thomas Goode's**, purveyor of china to the Queen. ⑤
Particularly notice the pair of seven foot ceramic ele-
phants in the windows; the Minton pottery made them for
the Paris Exhibitions in 1878 and 1889. Flowers are planted all around the shop. Go in and at least take a look.

NOON

T IME FOR YOUR LUNCH. Walk along the side of Goode's
store on South Street one block, turn right on
Waverton for about a block and a half, and turn left on
Hays Mews. The **Greenhouse**, where you made your ⑥
reservation, is just a few steps down the block.

The entrance to this restaurant is the prettiest in
London. Flower beds on either side of the canopied walk
take you into this romantic restaurant with its white linen
cloths and Victorian chairs. Lunch for two will be moderate in cost.

AFTERNOON

A FTER LUNCH, retrace your steps to South Audley.
Right on Waverton, left on South Street and right on
South Audley, remember? Two blocks further, you will
come to Mount Street.

Walk either right or left and look at the pink terra cotta
fronts from the late 19th century and the antique shops.
Every time I come to this corner, I am startled by the
beauty of the buildings. They are quite extraordinary.

Another two blocks north on South Audley will bring

⑦ you to **Grosvenor Square**, where you will find the United States Embassy with its huge, menacing eagle hovering overhead. I have never liked this Embassy because of its brutal look. The square has been associated with the United States since John Adams was America's first minister to Britain and lived at #9 on the square.

The area is known as Little America. Particularly notice the fine statue in memory of American President ⑧ **Franklin D. Roosevelt.** I have never been able to find out why the statue shows him standing, but I am sure there is a good reason.

Number 20 was headquarters for General Eisenhower in 1942 and 1944. Don't spend too much time around this rather sparse and uninviting square.

Walk back to Park Lane on Upper Brook Street to see great views of the city and the long terraces of homes. Turn right on Park Street to Lees Place to see a little cottage dated 1723 and Shepherd's Place with its antique street lamps.

⑨ NOW HEAD for the famous **Wallace Collection.** Continue north on Park Street which becomes Portman Street. Walk to the far (north) side of Portman square, turn right to Manchester Square where you will find the great Hertford House (Open weekdays 10 a.m. to 5 p.m.; Sunday noon-5 p.m., Free admission) which houses the Wallace Collection.

This great eighteenth century house has recently been transformed by American architect Rick Mather. He opened the atrium with a beautiful glass roof which brings light to both the courtyard and the "lower level" which I tend to call the "basement". The "lower level" now contains a lecture hall, temporary exhibition space and a library, plus a restaurant, the Café Bagatelle. The café is open during regular museum hours.

Galleries are also being transformed with the hanging

of heavy silk curtains and original fabrics on the walls.

This is the finest collection of French paintings, furniture and objects of art outside France; it is the most romantic house and art collection in the city.

Here you will find a wonderful series of rooms filled with sculpture, porcelain, furniture, paintings and armor in which you can wander to your heart's content and not worry about whether you have seen all the right things. Everything is lush and beautiful. The collection is particularly rich in ornate paintings by Boucher, Watteau and Fragonard.

It should now be late afternoon and time for tea. If you decide to bypass the museum's new café, take a cab to the **Hotel Dorchester Park Lane** you strolled past earlier. Their tea consists of little sandwiches and cakes and all manner of good things served in lovely surroundings. You might consider making this your light supper.

EVENING

DURING THE MIDDLE SUMMER MONTHS there are performances at the open air theatre in **Regent's Park.** What could be more romantic than watching a production of *A Midsummer's Night Dream* in the rose gardens of the park?

If you have followed my earlier suggestions, you will have arranged for tickets for the park performance. Relax and enjoy the evening and think about your long, meandering boat trip planned for tomorrow.

Romantic
Day 2

Hampton Court Road

Cafeteria

Lion Gates

Maze

Restaurant

Wilderness

Trophy Gates

Start

Tudor Tennis Court

BROAD WALK

Palace
and State
Apartments

Lower Orangery

Fountain Court

Great Vine

Thames

Privy Garden

Tijou Screen

N

MAP OF HAMPTON COURT

LONDON ▶

RIVER THAMES

Hampton
Court

THAMES RIVER
ROUTE
TO HAMPTON COURT

DAY 2

Highlights: Westminster Pier, Thames River and Hampton Court, open mid-March to mid-October.

Reservations: Departure from Westminster Pier at 11 a.m., 11:15 a.m., and 12 noon. Telephone (020 7930-2062 or 020 7930-4721. Double- check sailing times since they are subject to change. The trip takes from three to four hours.

Less romantic, but faster: Trains run frequently from Waterloo Station. Telephone (01603)764-776. London Transport also runs frequent buses from Victoria Coach Station, southwest of Victoria Station. Telephone 020/7730-3466.

Dinner reservations: Bombay Brasserie, Bailey Hotel, 1 Courtfield Close, Courtfield Road, South Kensington. Telephone 020 7835-1669.

MORNING

TODAY, IF YOU TAKE THE ROMANTIC ROAD, you are going to follow the path of kings down London's main highway and spend the afternoon in a royal palace and garden. The highway is the **Thames River** and your destination is **Hampton Court**, the palace built by Cardinal Wolsey, Henry VIII and William and Mary.

The monarchs and courtiers of England went to this idyllic spot by way of the river to spend weeks in pleasure and parties or to escape the various plagues which infested the city.

This morning you will take that same trip, leaving from **Westminster Pier**. The 21-mile trip takes about three hours and 45 minutes. I suggest you plan to take the boat to Hampton Court and return by train or bus from Hampton. Sailing schedules are always subject to weather and are only operative in the summer months. The boats leave from the pier at 10 a.m., 10:30 a.m., 11 a.m., and 12 noon. They return from Hampton at 3, 4 and 5 p.m.

I suggest you leave on the 10 a.m. boat.

I cannot imagine a more romantic trip than following this route, first past Parliament and the London bridges; alongside great country houses, the park at Richmond, Kew Gardens and finally Hampton, itself.

Plan to visit the **State Apartments** when you first arrive at **Hampton Court.** They are open March to late October on Mondays from 10:15 a.m. to 4:30 p.m. Late October to late March, Tuesday to Sunday, 9:30 a.m. to 6 p.m. Monday 10:15 a.m. to 6 p.m.

SEE   The red brick **Palace** is complicated; you do not have
DETAIL   the days you need to explore it on your own. Besides, you
MAP
want time to roam the gardens, the maze, the tennis court, and all the other wonders on the grounds.

Let your imagination roam as you, too, walk up the **King's Staircase** with its incredible wall and ceiling paintings. The Wolsey rooms are at the top of the stairs; be sure to look out the windows in the various rooms to see magnificent views of the gardens. I will not attempt to describe the paintings, furniture and other objects you will see.

Remember to look in every direction: on the walls, on the floors and especially overhead. The **Great Hall** built by Henry VIII in 1531-36 has one of the finest hammer beam roofs in the world.

As you leave the magnificent living and sleeping quarters of the royal families, you will descend to **Anne Boleyn's Gateway**. There you will find the King's Beer Cellar which will give you some idea of what was involved in servicing a palace with more than 500 guests. Then come the Tudor kitchens and serving areas. Check out the audio guides as well as the costumed guided tours.

NOON

YOU WILL EMERGE into the **gardens.** It is time to visit the tearoom for lunch, a sweet and or a "cuppa"tea. This is a pleasant and convenient place to eat and rest before exploring the gardens.

AFTERNOON

THE **BROAD WALK** runs across the front of the palace. Visit the nearby indoor tennis court. I was lucky enough one day to see men playing on the courts with the old, short handled rackets of Henry VIII's day. They have more modern courts on the grounds, but these old ones are very special.

The **Privy gardens** are on the south side of the palace near a fine screen by Jean Tijou and the knot garden of herbs. Incidentally, knot gardens are defined as 'neatly trimmed plants intricately laid out to form simple or complex patterns'.

Further on is the **Great Vine** planted in 1768. Look for the Lower Orangery with the famous tempera paintings by Mantegna.

On the north side of the palace is the wilderness and the famous **Maze.** I think part of the fun is working through it by yourself, getting lost and finally deciding you are there for life. In a 1918 guide book, I read that you take the first two right turns and then left at every next turn. I do not know if that still works, but you might want to try it.

On my first trip I vowed to walk the maze come hell or high water. No hell, but lots of water. It poured rain. But I walked it with my umbrella held, not only over my head,

but up above the hedges. They are planted so close together I could not fit the umbrella between them. Someone in
a helicopter would have seen a bright red umbrella making its way through this maze of plantings

I assure you, you will find your way out. They never
leave anyone in it overnight. If you get claustrophobic,
just signal the 'maze keeper' who sits on top of a tall lad-
der surveying the scene and he will send help.

A train will take you back from Hampton Court to the
Waterloo station.

EVENING

Y OU SHOULD GET BACK to London in time for dinner at
the **Bombay Brasserie** in the Bailey Hotel. This sky-
lighted pavilion with its wicker furniture, potted plants
and romantic lighting will serve dinner for two for a moderate cost. Its splendid menu includes such delicacies as
crisp Indian bread, stuffed quail, curries, a wonderfully
colored mango sherbet and Kingfisher beer made in India.

Relax and enjoy this pretty place and prepare for
tomorrow's picnic in the park and a final event at the
Tower of London as it closes for the night.

DAY 3

Highlights: Piccadilly Circus, Burlington Arcade, St.
James's Park, Queen's Gallery, Royal Mews, and Tower of
London for Ceremony of the Keys.

Reservations: Ritz Hotel for tea. Telephone 020 7907
2618. For dinner: Butler's Wharf Chop House 020 7403
3414. Make an early reservation because you have to be at
the Tower of London at 9:30 p.m. This restaurant is across
the river from the Tower of London. Plan to take a cab
from the restaurant to the tower.

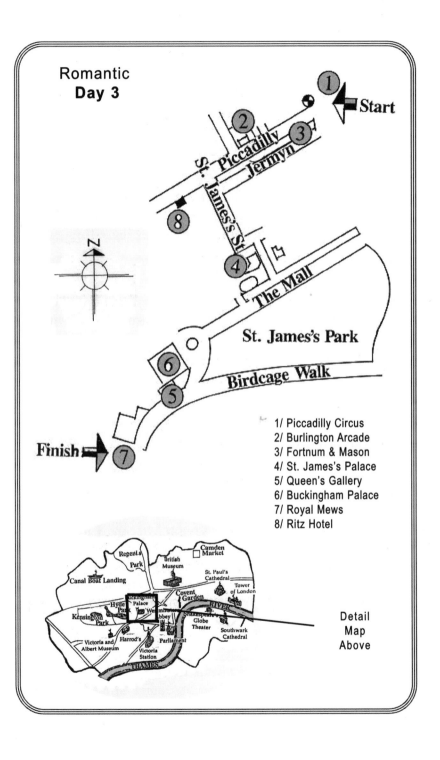

Romantic
Day 3

Start

1/ Piccadilly Circus
2/ Burlington Arcade
3/ Fortnum & Mason
4/ St. James's Palace
5/ Queen's Gallery
6/ Buckingham Palace
7/ Royal Mews
8/ Ritz Hotel

Piccadilly

Jermyn

St. James's St.

The Mall

St. James's Park

Birdcage Walk

Finish

Detail
Map
Above

Ceremony of the Keys at the Tower of London. At least two months in advance, write for free tickets, to: Ceremony of the Keys, Waterloo Block, Tower of London, London EC3N 4AB to request a specific date. An international reply coupon (from your post office) must be enclosed. Give your name, alternative dates desired and the number of people in your party. Include a self-addressed envelope, stamped with British stamps or two International Reply coupons. You can get these from your post office.

MORNING

① YOU WILL START TODAY at **Piccadilly Circus** about 10 a.m. This is where Regent Street comes to an abrupt and awkward end; not at all where it was supposed to stop. But end it does, where about five or six streets pour into this busy intersection.

Right smack in the middle is a fountain once topped by the figure of **Eros**, the goddess of love. She has recently been moved to the side of the Circus in front of the Criterion Theatre. The statue is officially known as the Angel of Christian Charity and is a memorial to the philanthropist Lord Shaftesbury. But for our purposes Eros, with his little winged cap, remains a romantic symbol.

Make your way down Piccadilly, past the Royal Academy to the **Burlington Arcade.** It comes as some-② what of a surprise to find this glass-domed arcade was built in 1819. It is still patrolled by beadles, ex-soldiers of the 10th Hussar, dressed in their uniforms and prepared to enforce the rules. Whistling, for some strange reason, is still against the law.

Your purchases might include a brocade vest, cashmere sweater, linen hankie or a piece of jewelry. Even here the shops change from time to time.

Walk west on Piccadilly to St. James Street and one

block to your left to **Jermyn Street** and turn left. Walk up one side of this street and back the other. All along the way are the old and still very active shops which have been there for many years.

Floris, purveyor of scents to the royal family, still sells its perfume and real bristle brushes; **Paxton and Whitehead** reaches out to you with both sight and smell with its cheeses and hams; and **Dunhill's** attracts with its tobacco and other appurtenances.

And finally you are at the back door of **Fortnum and** ③ **Mason's.** Wander through and pick up some of the prepared foods, bread and a sweet to take to St. James's Park for a picnic with the ducks and swans.

Walk back to St. James's Street, turn left and walk on down to the park. You will pass some of London's oldest shops, Locks for hats and Lobbs for boots and some of the great palaces, St. James's and Marlborough House.

NOON

One of the great treasures of London is its green spaces and one of my favorites is little **St. James's Park** ④ with its pretty lake and wildlife.

Find a folding chair or a bench and sit in the sun, feed the ducks, eat your lunch and enjoy the beauty of the park and its people. An attendant will stop and collect a few pence rent for use of the chair.

AFTERNOON

AFTER AN HOUR IN THE PARK, it should be around 1:30 or 2 p.m. Walk up the Birdcage Walk to the **Queen's Gallery**. Open daily 10 a.m. to 5:30 p.m. Special ⑤ exhibitions from the royal collections are often on display. The galleries were remodeled in 2002 for Queen Elizabeth's Golden Jubilee celebration.

The nearby royal stables called the **Royal Mews** are ⑦

open daily from 11 a.m. to 3:15 p.m., sometimes with and sometimes without the horses, include the harness rooms and coach houses. Of special interest is the Glass Coach which you will remember from The wedding and the Gold State Coach used at every coronation since 1820.

(6)   Walk around **Buckingham Palace**. This is not the time to see the changing of the guard, but you will see the guard at work. Amble back around the palace and up The Mall, to St. James's Palace and Clarence House.

     Walk up St. James's Street to Piccadilly again and by

(8) now it should be 4 p.m. and time for tea in the **Palm Court** of the **Ritz Hotel**. The hotel is just to your left.

EVENING

B ack to your hotel for a brief rest before your dinner at **Butlers Wharf.** Take a cab. The restaurant is run by Sir Terence Conran and features great views across the river to the Tower, plus outdoor eating places in good weather.

See Tower of London Map

     You need to be at the entrance to the **Tower of London** for the Ceremony of the Keys by 9:30 p.m. This ancient ceremony has taken place each evening for nearly 700 years.

     The Chief Warder of the Tower locks the gates and presents the keys to the Resident Governor. The words remain the same, except for the change in the name of the monarch:

Halt! Who comes there?

The Keys

Whose Keys?

Queen Elizabeth's Keys.

The lighted tower, the old and famous ceremony, and the costumed participants who are part of this enduring tradition are symbolic of the long and often romantic legacy of this city.

As you leave the tower and hail a cab to return to your hotel, you will know you have been a part of this romantic tradition.

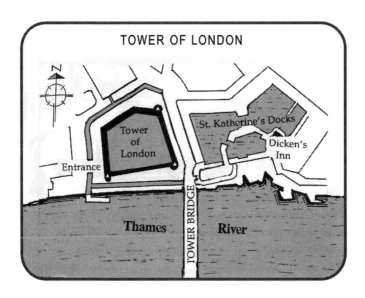

Royal **Day 1**

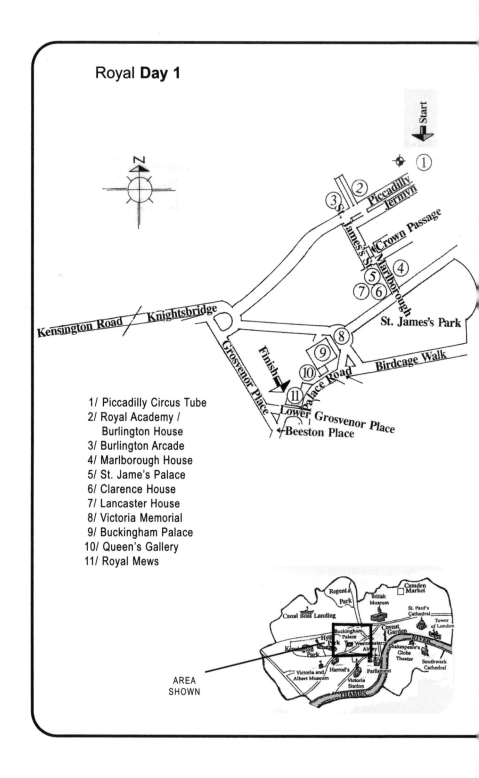

1/ Piccadilly Circus Tube
2/ Royal Academy /
   Burlington House
3/ Burlington Arcade
4/ Marlborough House
5/ St. Jame's Palace
6/ Clarence House
7/ Lancaster House
8/ Victoria Memorial
9/ Buckingham Palace
10/ Queen's Gallery
11/ Royal Mews

AREA
SHOWN

ROYAL LONDON

Follow the track of English royalty
and their lifestyles, past and present.
Get a feel for their extraordinary life

M ANY VISITORS come to London like the pussycat in the nursery rhyme, *To look at the Queen.* Chances are most of us will not even get a glimpse of the royal family, but you can visit the royal palaces, gardens and memorials, and if timed right, you may be in town for one of the grand state events.

The British monarchy endows the United Kingdom with more than pomp and pageantry. It has provided stability and a sense of unity for a commonwealth which has undergone enormous changes during the centuries. It is a rare and unique phenomenon.

During the past few years, the royal family has had more than its share of sorrows and tragedies: a major fire at Windsor Castle, divorces, scandals, illnesses and, finally, the tragic death of Princess Diana in an automobile accident on August 31, 1997.

Windsor has been restored; the divorces and scandals took a back seat to sorrow over the princess' death, celebrations and new buildings and renovations in celebration of the Millennium and the Queen's Jubilee year have changed London and environs tremendously. And the monarchy continues.

If you are bound and determined to see the royals, check *The Times*, *The Standard* or the *Daily Telegraph* for listings of their public appearances.

Other opportunities to view members of the royal family occur on state occasions.

The State Opening of Parliament usually takes place late in October. The Queen rides through the streets in one of the state carriages to preside at the opening. Trooping the Colours takes place in mid-June and honors the queen's official birthday. She rides horseback to the Horse Guard's Parade on Whitehall and later appears on the balcony at Buckingham Palace. On Remembrance Sunday, the Sunday closest to November 11, the Queen remembers the heroes of the two World Wars by placing wreaths on the Cenotaph in Whitehall.

Or, if you are famous enough in your own country or have served the Commonwealth in some noteworthy way, you may be invited to one of the three garden parties held each year at Buckingham Palace. About 10,000 people attend each of these galas; it is considered a great honor to be invited.

But finally in 1993 the palace, or at least parts of it, were opened to the public daily in August and September from 9:30 to 4 p.m. Advance booking is necessary: telephone 020 7321 2233 or book on line at www.royal.gov.uk. Tickets are sold from a booth in Green Park...long lines and a long wait. Get your tickets in advance.

Barring all these opportunities, you can still see magnificent sights and get a feel for the extraordinary life of the royals in and near London by visiting their homes, gardens and art collections.

DAY 1

Highlights: Changing of the Guard at Buckingham Palace, Royal Academy of Art, Queen's Gallery and Kensington Palace.

Reservations: Dinner at the Ritz Hotel Restaurant, Piccadilly. Telephone 020 7907 2681

MORNING

SINCE THE CHANGING of the guard does not take place until 11:30 a.m., start the day by visiting some of the nearby royal buildings and shops. Take the tube or cab to **Piccadilly Circus**, where you will walk down Piccadilly ① to the **Burlington House and Arcade**. The word, Piccadilly, came from the name of a tailor who made the 'pickadillies', the famous ruff collars worn by Elizabethan dandies.

The Earl of Burlington began the **Burlington House** in ① 1664; it was converted to the Royal Academy of Arts in 1768. It contains magnificent paintings, furniture and the only Michelangelo sculpture in England, his unfinished *Madonna and Child*. Summer exhibitions have been held here annually for over 200 years, from May through September.

The Academy opens daily from 10 a.m. to 6 p.m., but the hours for the Summer Exhibition change, so check the daily papers. Adjacent to the Burlington House is the **Burlington Arcade**, a covered shopping arcade built in ③ 1819.

After looking at these charming shops, walk down Piccadilly to St. James's Street, turn left, walk one block to Jermyn Street, and turn left again. You will find a number of shops which bear the seal indicating they serve the royal family, including **Floris**, the shop of perfumes established in 1730.

Walk back to St. James's Street and turn left; you will pass **Lobb's,** shoemakers since the 18th century and the hatters, Lock and Company, in business since 1700. **Berry Bros. and Rudd**, wine merchants, have been on their site since 1680.

A slight jog to your left and St. James's Street becomes Marlborough Road. On your left is **Marlborough House**, designed by Sir Christopher Wren ④ in 1709. It now provides offices for the Commonwealth Foundation and Secretariat.

Next to it is the **Queen's Chapel** designed by architect Inigo Jones. It is not usually open to the public except by written application, but Sunday services are held here from Easter to the end of July. Attending this service is a very formal and special treat. When I went to a Sunday service one morning, I felt that I was surrounded by retainers of the royal family, very carefully and correctly dressed with their hats, gloves and well-tailored suits.

⑤ On your right, opposite Marlborough House, is **St. James's Palace**, once the home of the royal families. Remember, ambassadors are accredited to the Court of St. James! The St. James's Chapel Royal is open for services on Sundays from the first of October to Good Friday.

⑥ Next to the palace is **Clarence House**. The white stucco house was once the home of Queen Elizabeth, the Queen 'Mum'. She died in 2002 at the age of 101. The house is now the official London residence for The Prince of Wales. The house is occasionally open to the public.

You can walk down The Mall and around Clarence house to the courtyard of St. James's Palace.

⑦ **Lancaster House** is across the road. It was built for the Duke of York in 1825 and has been the location of many great parties. It is not open to the public.

A S YOU ARRIVE at **The Mall**, turn right, but look to your left to see the full extent of this ceremonial road: the processional way for royalty on state occasions. It starts at the Admiralty Arch at Trafalgar, moves past Carlton House Terrace, Marlborough House, St. James's Palace, Clarence House and on to Buckingham Palace.

⑧ As you turn right, you will see the **Victoria Memorial** straight ahead and **Buckingham Palace**, just beyond. The Queen Victoria white marble memorial was completed in 1910. The seated monarch is surrounded by statues of Truth, Motherhood and Justice. It is also one of the best places from which to see the Changing of the Guard. You will probably find a number of people already perched on it, trying to get a good vantage point.

Buckingham Palace was begun by the Duke of
Buckingham in 1703, taken over by George III and
expanded by George IV and the great architect John Nash.
Nash's work was brilliant but vastly over budget and the
design work was completed by another architect.

Nash's most embarrassing mistake was his great arch-
way, known as the Marble Arch, which now stands at the
corner of Oxford Street and Edgeware Road. It had to be
towed away from its original site when they realized it
was too narrow for the king's coach.

Queen Victoria, with her nine children, added a number of additions to the palace. She was finally satisfied
with its present 600 rooms. 600 Rooms!

Here you are at 11:30 a.m., waiting for the number one
tourist attraction of the city of London, the **Changing
of the Guard**. I will be very candid with you: this is one
of my least favorite events in London, primarily because
it is almost impossible to see or hear. The crowds are
enormous, the noise of the traffic is deafening and crossing the street is impossible.

Two small pieces of advice: get as close to the center
of the main gate as possible and climb up on the Victoria
Memorial to look over people's heads if you can. At about
11:10 a.m., a contingent of the old guard parade in
Ambassador's Court at St. James's Palace and move
toward the Palace. They join the old Palace guard at the
left of the center gates about 11:25 a.m.

The new guard, along with a band, march either from
the Chelsea Barracks, or in bad weather, from the nearby
Wellington Barracks. As they arrive at the Palace, officers
of the old and new advance, touch left hands as symbols
of the handing over of the keys and the guard is changed.
Eight men detach themselves to relieve the sentries at St.
James's Palace, Clarence House and Buckingham Palace.

At this time, music is played in the forecourt. The old
guard moves out the center gates about 12:10 with the
band playing, to return to the barracks; the new guard

goes on duty at Buckingham Palace. A small detachment of guards with a group of drummers leaves by the right gate to relieve the guards at St. James's Palace and Clarence House.

And that is the Changing of the Guard. I wish you luck and hope you can see at least some part of what is an impressive ceremony and/or visit the Palace if you are lucky enough to get tickets.

NOON

GETTING OUT OF THE CROWD is no mean feat because you have to cross traffic no matter which way you go. Since I want you to come back here to see the Queen's Gallery and the Royal Mews after lunch, I will suggest some nearby pubs or restaurants. You may choose to go back up the Mall to Marlborough Road, retracing your steps of this morning.

Walk up Marlborough Road and almost straight ahead, a bit to your right is **Crown Passage,** just off Pall Mall. Here you will find pleasant eating establishments. Or you can continue up **St. James's Street** (remember it is an extension of Marlborough Road) to Jermyn Street, turn right and walk on to the **Red Lion Pub** or to **Fortnum and Mason's** for lunch.

Another more expensive place is the **Goring Hotel** on Beeston Place, just off Lower Grosvenor Place, behind the Royal Mews. They have both a set and a la carte menu. This is a very expensive restaurant, but after all, this is Royal London. Service is excellent; the room with its chandeliers, sheer Roman curtains and aqua velvet chairs is lovely. They offer a trolley with a large selection of appetizers ranging from fresh fruits to pates and mayonnaise eggs, a British favorite I don't quite understand. Telephone 020 7396-9000.

AFTERNOON

R ETRACE YOUR STEPS after lunch to Buckingham Palace
and the **Queen's Gallery,** which is alongside the ⑩
palace. Watch for the signs. It is open daily 10 a.m. to
5:30 p.m. The gallery contains special exhibitions drawn
from the Royal Collection, which is one of the greatest art
collections in the world. Check the newspapers for information on the current exhibition, but no matter what it is,
go to see it. It will be magnificent.

Walk down the road to the **Royal Mews**. These stables ⑪
are open from 11 a.m. to 3 p.m. They contain the horses,
coach rooms and the state carriages including the glass
coach used by Princess Diana and Prince Charles later by
Prince Andrew and Sarah Ferguson; the Gold Coach used
for coronations, and the Irish Coach in which the queen
rides to the state opening of Parliament.

At this point, start walking up Grosvenor Place toward
Hyde Park or hail a cab to take you to **Kensington Palace.**
They can drop you on Kensington Road at the Broad
Walk. Or you can walk through Hyde Park and Kensington
Gardens, if you want a very long walk. Use the cab. It will
be a short and inexpensive ride, saving your feet for bet-
ter things.

Walk up the Broad Walk to the **Palace.** Princess
Margaret, Princess Diana and Prince Charles and about 11
other members of the royal family lived here at one time.
The palace is open daily from 10 a.m. to 5 p.m. The **State
Apartments** where Prince Charles and Diana lived are not
open to the public since other royals such as the Duke and
Duchess of Kent now live there.

Christopher Wren was the prime architect after its purchase in 1689 by William III. Kensington Palace is much
associated with Queen Victoria who was born and grew up
there until the chilly night when the Archbishop of
Canterbury came to tell her she was Queen of England.

Walk past the sunken gardens to the entry to the apartments. A multi-language sound guide is available in

English, French, German, Spanish and Italian. The guide is included in the ticket price.

There is so much to see that I will mention only a "Few of my Favorite Things." Do use the sound guide...it will be very helpful.

Go up the **King's Staircase** to his apartments. This grand staircase has masks and sea horses on the lower part of the walls, but the upper section is covered with six-teenth-century Italian illusionist paintings. Onlookers painted on the ceiling watch you as you wend your way up this staircase. The **Presence Chamber,** where the king received visitors, is hung with rare seventeenth-century Italian embroideries. Note the ceiling showing the sun god, Apollo, in his chariot. And the mantel decorated by the famous carver, Grinling Gibbons, covered with birds, flowers, fruit and cherubs' heads.

On to the Privy Chamber with its great ceiling show-ing Mars and Minerva and into the **Cupola Room**, the principal state room in the palace. Follow along, looking at the labels if you need help, but mostly, just get the feel-ing of this very human royal residence. Walk through the Cupola room where Queen Victoria was baptized, the Victorian Rooms and the Queen's apartments. On to the King's Drawing room and Gallery with its great Italian paintings and another magnificent Kent ceiling.

Return to the ground floor to see a collection of court dress and an exhibition of the clothing worn by the late Diana, Princess of Wales.

As you leave the palace, go to the nearby **Orangery** , built as a summer house for Queen Anne. Here is the first place you can sit and drink tea, have a nice lunch and look at the Grinling Gibbons carvings and statues surrounding you. This is a very favorite place of mine.

EVENING

By now both you and the day should be fading. Try to go back to your hotel for a rest. Tonight it is dinner at

NOON

THERE ARE A NUMBER of good restaurants and pubs on Eton High Street. **Sir Christopher Wren's Old House** on Thames Street in the little town of Windsor was built and lived in by Christopher Wren. The **Castle Hotel** on High Street, just opposite the castle, has a restaurant, bar and coffee shop.

AFTERNOON

DEPENDING ON HOW LONG you stay at Windsor and your transportation, you should be back in London in late afternoon, in time for a nice cream tea at the **Dorchester Hotel** on Park Lane. It may not be quite the same as tea with the royals, but it is quite nice.

EVENING

Dinner at **Claridge's Hotel** on Brook Street tonight, a favorite with royalty since Queen Victoria's time. During World War II, it served as a palace for three monarchs in exile. It is expensive as you might guess, but distinctly royal.

Get a good rest, because we are going out of town again tomorrow.

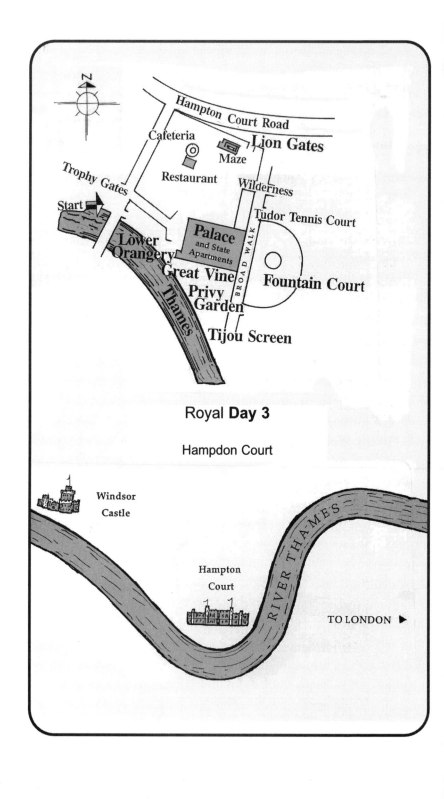

Royal **Day 3**

Hampdon Court

DAY 3

Highlights: Hampton Court and the Thames River.

Reservations: Tickets for the Royal Shakespeare Company. Check newspapers or magazines for schedule. The Practical Information chapter provides help with ordering theatre tickets.

Today your Royal London tour takes you to **Hampton Court**. You can go by way of the Thames River from Westminster Pier as the monarchs used to go, or you can train from Waterloo Station or take a bus. From Richmond station (District Line and SouthWest Trains) take R68 bus and from Hounslow East (Piccadilly Line) take the 111 bus. The river trip takes almost three hours, but it is an elegant and leisurely way to travel to Hampton. You can return on any of the public transportation routes.

If Windsor was built as a castle and a fortress, Hampton Court with its gardens, galleries and ornate buildings was built as a pleasure palace. It was begun in 1514 by Cardinal Wolsey, surrendered by him to Henry VIII and added on to by William III, who hired Wren to design and build additional wings to the palace.

Open mid-March to mid-October daily from 10:15 a.m. to 4:30 p.m.; October through March, 9:30 a.m. to 4:30 p.m., Mondays 10:15 a.m. to 6:30 p.m.

Closed Dec. 24-26. There is some variation in open times for the apartments, tennis court and banqueting house. Check when you arrive.

The State Apartments are magnificent, but if the weather is nice, it is the gardens you particularly want to visit. Pick up a map when you arrive, but be sure to wander through the formal and not-so-formal gardens, see the Great Vine and the tennis courts and work your way through the maze.

The State Apartments are filled with much of the original furniture and decorations and contain about 500 paintings. You will follow a path through the apartments.

Begin by walking up the **King's Staircase**. Note the walls and ceilings. Look in every direction: at the floors, the walls, the ceilings decorated by the artist Verrio. All the rooms contain glorious objects; the Italian paintings are among the finest.

The **Prince of Wales Presence Chamber** contains many of the best Italian paintings. Also notice the fine tapestries everywhere. Lely's portraits of the ladies of Charles II's court, the Windsor Beauties hang in the Communication Gallery. The ghost of Queen Catherine Howard is said to still walk in the Haunted Gallery.

Henry VIII's Great Watching Chamber is hung with Flemish tapestries. The **Great Hall** built by Henry VIII has one of the finest hammer-beam roofs in the world and wonderful Brussels tapestries.

The Tudor kitchens, with their huge fireplaces and dark hallways, take you at last to the Wren Fountain Court and the Chapel.

NOON

THE VISIT TO HAMPTON COURT is an all-day excursion, but there is a restaurant on the grounds near the Maze, and small kiosks for food near the entrance as well as a coffee shop near the Tudor Kitchens.

The **Tiltyard Restaurant** in the palace gardens has a coffee bar, a buffet restaurant and outside terrace. On Sundays they have waitress-served lunches. Spaces are limited so make a reservation. Call 020 8943 3666.

EVENING

TONIGHT when you return to London, have a rest, eat at your hotel and go see whatever the **Royal Shakespeare Company** is doing wherever they are doing it.

They are always magnificent. No member of the royal family ever saw better theatre than you will see with this company.

F OR THE PAST THREE DAYS you have trod the paths of royalty. You have visited their palaces, seen their royal coaches, art collections, shops and parks and attended their theatres, ballet and opera.

It may not be the same as wearing the crown, but it should have given you a taste of the royal life.

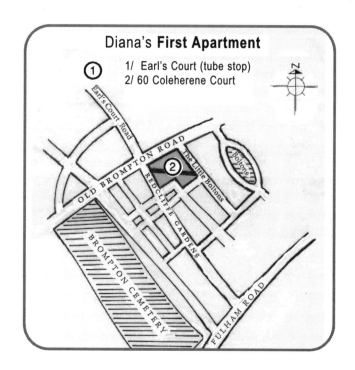

Diana's **First Apartment**

① 1/ Earl's Court (tube stop)
2/ 60 Coleherene Court

IN THE FOOTSTEPS
OF PRINCESS DIANA

A special tour
for Diana fans

F OR THOSE OF YOU who want to visit some of the places
made special by the late Princess Diana, the following
are a few suggestions.

In 1979, one of the best-known addresses in London
② was **60 Coleherne Court**, Diana's first place of her own.
Bought with money inherited from her American great-
grandmother, Fanny Work, the four-bedroom flat sported
red wallpaper and a modern kitchen. Diana's First
① Apartment is located just south of **Earl's Court,** between
The Little Boltons and **Redcliffe Gardens** roads.

Diana shared her flat with three friends: Carolyn

Pride, a student at the Royal College of Music; Virginia Pitman, who worked at Asprey's, the British version of New York's Tiffany's; and Anne Bolton, who worked for an estate agent. Needless to say, Diana had the largest bedroom.

Diana used the cooking skills she had picked up at a Cordon Bleu school, but limited her output to chocolate roulades and Russian borscht soup.

This was a happy time for Diana, marred only by the loss of some of her jewelry when the apartment was burglarized. The girls became part of the group known as the Sloane Rangers, a young group which shopped on Sloane Street, went to weekly dinner parties and spent weekends in the country.

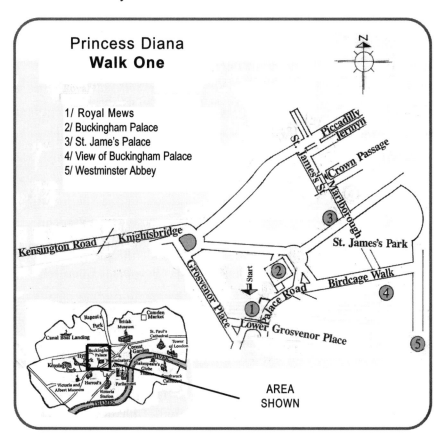

Princess Diana
Walk One

1/ Royal Mews
2/ Buckingham Palace
3/ St. Jame's Palace
4/ View of Buckingham Palace
5/ Westminster Abbey

AREA
SHOWN

At this time in her life, Diana taught at the Young England Kindergarten at St. Saviour's Church on the corner of St. George's Square and Lupus Street in Pimlico, to the west of Pimlico tube station and west of the Tate Gallery.

WALK ONE

① AT THE ROYAL MEWS, you will find the **ceremonial glass carriage** which carried Diana and Prince Charles to their wedding at St. Paul's Cathedral.

② Just beyond the Mews you come to **Buckingham Palace**, where Diana stayed during the weeks before her wedding and to which she returned after the ceremony for lobster, strawberries and champagne.

③ Continue east on the Mall to **Clarence House** and St. James's Palace, where Diana's body laid during the days before her funeral. Incidentally, St. James's Palace is Prince Charles' home during his stays in London.

Cut through St. James's Park and walk over the bridge to see the finest view of Buckingham Palace.

④ Then east on Birdcage Road to the end, turn right to **Westminster Abbey**, where Diana's funeral was held in 1997.

WALK TWO

ANOTHER WALK IS in the Kensington area. Here you can visit **Kensington Palace** where Diana and her family lived on three floors on the north side of the palace. You are not allowed to visit these particular rooms. I can tell you a bit about them, however.

Diana did a great deal of redecorating after the Queen gave her and Prince Charles their two apartments. Walls were painted peach, woodwork painted white in the dining room; down-filled sofas were covered with pale salmon silk and a Broadwood grand piano was played by Diana and other guests such as Elton John and Vladimir Horowitz. It is possible that you will find bouquets of flowers still being left at the great gate on the south side of the palace.

Since Diana's death, Kensington Palace underwent a massive restoration. The Palace was reopened the summer of 1998. Tour guides are available, but not to any of the private quarters as I wrote earlier.

The two princes, William and Harry, were born at nearby **St. Mary's Hospital.** Walk east on Craven Hill Road, which becomes Praed Street, to find the hospital. Some years later the princess officially opened the Rodney Porter Ward hospice at this hospital. The two princes attended a local boys' school, just north of Kensington Palace, the **Wetherby School** in Pembroke Square in Notting Hill. Walk north from Notting Hill Gate to Pembroke Square.

Even further north in this same Kensington area, walk or take Bus 52 north on Kensington Road to Lancaster Road. At 111 - 117 Lancaster Road you will find **The Lighthouse**, the largest center in Europe for people affected with HIV and AIDS. This was one of Princess Diana's favorite London charities, which she visited and supported.

There is a **cafe** with a lovely garden with fountains and summertime tables. Tea is served throughout the day.

SOME OF PRINCESS DIANA'S FAVORITE PLACES

San Lorenzo at 22 Beauchamp Place in Knightsbridge, just south of Harrod's, was generally considered her favorite restaurant. This Italian restaurant is pricey but has good food; its one drawback is that it takes no credit cards. The restaurant specializes in food from Tuscany and the Piedmont, including homemade fettucini, risotto with asparagus, and partridge in white-wine sauce.

It is popular so that reservations are sensible. Call 020/ 7584 - 1074. It is open Monday through Saturday from 12:30 to 3 p.m. and 7:30 to 11:30 p.m.

Diana's **Favorite Places**

1/ Beauchamp Place
2/ Harrod's
3/ Sloan Square
4/ Sloane Street

①   On **Beauchamp Place** are a number of shops she visited, including **Caroline Charles** at number 56 - 57 and **Bruce Oldfield** at number 27 for womenswear; and **Bill Bentley's** wine bar at number 31. I have to admit that these places may have changed; the "trendy" spots change regularly.

②   And of course you will want to visit **Harrod's Department Store**, owned by Mohammed al-Fayed, the father of Dodi al-Fayed, who was killed with the princess in that terrible car crash. There was a temporary memorial to the two young people set up in the store; plans were afoot to make it a permanent memorial. Harrod's is at 135 Brompton Road, between Hans Crescent and Hans Road.

③   Take a short cab ride from Harrod's to **Sloane Square** where you can visit two of her favorite department stores: **Peter Jones** and the **General Trading Company**, where

Princess Diana registered just like any other bride.

If you have the energy, walk north on **Sloane Street** to ④ feel the general atmosphere of the street that became the beat for the Sloane Rangers. It will not be difficult to spot the places Diana and her friends would have visited, including the famous **Cadogan Hotel.** Every famous name is located on this street: Prada, Armani, Ungaro, Valentino, Yves Saint Laurent, Dolce & Gabbana, Hermes, Chanel, Vuitton and Christian Lacroix. I think it is safe to say that she would have visited most of them.

Just north of Picadilly Circus on Regent Street is the famous jeweler **Garrard**, where Prince Charles bought Princess Diana's engagement ring, a large central sapphire surrounded by eighteen diamonds.

A ND FINALLY you will want to make a special trip to **St. Paul's Cathedral** to remember that glorious moment in the life of this princess: her wedding day on July 29, 1981.

Television sets were turned on all over the world so that everyone could share her three-and-one-half minute walk down the aisle on her father's arm; the glorious music by the famous boys' choir, three orchestras, the Bach Choir and the soprano Kiri Te Kanawa and the return to Buckingham Palace in the glass coach by Prince Charles and Diana, then the highest-ranking princess in the land.

Perhaps this is the way you want to remember her.

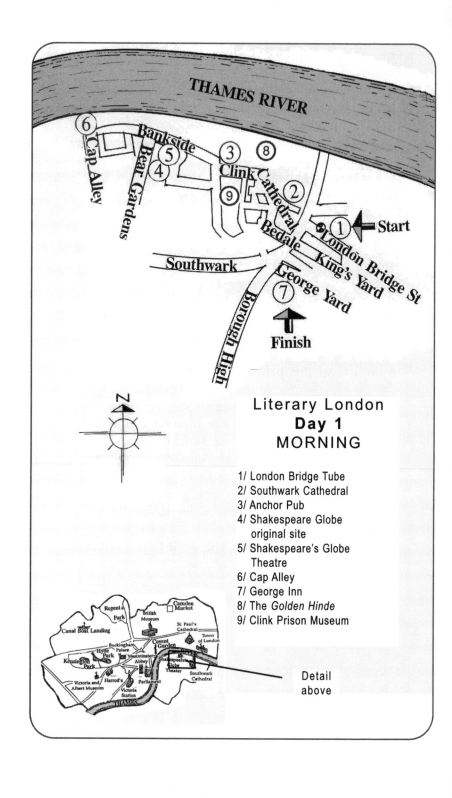

THAMES RIVER

6 Cap Alley
Bankside
Bear Gardens
5
4
3
8
Clink
Cathedral
9
2
1 ← Start
London Bridge St
Bedale
King's Yard
Southwark
George Yard
7
Borough High
Finish

N

Literary London
Day 1
MORNING

1/ London Bridge Tube
2/ Southwark Cathedral
3/ Anchor Pub
4/ Shakespeare Globe
   original site
5/ Shakespeare's Globe
   Theatre
6/ Cap Alley
7/ George Inn
8/ The *Golden Hinde*
9/ Clink Prison Museum

Regent's Park
British Museum
Camden Market
St. Paul's Cathedral
Canal Boat Landing
Covent Garden
Tower of London
Buckingham Palace
Hyde Park
Westminster Abbey
Kensington Park
Shakespeare's Globe Theater
Southwark Cathedral
Victoria and Albert Museum
Harrod's
Parliament
Victoria Station
THAMES

Detail
above

LITERARY
LONDON

Trod the cobblestones where almost
every important writer in the English language
has lived, worked or studied

LONDON IS THE BIRTHPLACE of English literature and the mother of English and American writers. Almost every important writer in the English language has lived, worked or studied in London some time during his or her life. Many of London's more than 600 famous blue plaques identify the houses of the famous and appear on buildings which housed writers. With a little help in planning and a vivid imagination you can visit and recreate the London of Chaucer, Shakespeare and Virginia Woolf.

In the 14th century, Geoffrey Chaucer's pilgrims lead the way not only to the Canterbury Cathedral but to the literary tradition which followed. Their journey began at the Tabard Inn in Southwark on the south bank of the Thames.

Southwark also became home to Shakespeare and his great circular theatres, the wooden O's. His earthy plays were performed for the working people standing in the pits of such theatres as the Globe, the Hope, the Rose and the Star. Across the river, John Donne was writing his love poems, first secular and later sacred, as he assumed the role of Dean of St. Paul's Cathedral.

The Great Fire of 1666, which destroyed much of central London, was reported in the diaries of Samuel Pepys and John Evelyn, remarkable accounts not only of the fire but more importantly of the times and the people.

By the 16th century and the Age of Reason, Alexander Pope was writing satire; Dr. Samuel Johnson was sitting in the Cheshire Cheese pub with his literary compatriots and working on his famous Dictionary.

In the 18th century, while Keats and Wordsworth were living in Hampstead and Westminster and writing about fair England and nightingales, Charles Dickens, the reformer and novelist, was writing about slums, prisons, thieves and London's "pea soupers" (his name for the London fogs).

The 20th century brought the Bloomsbury group together with Virginia Woolf and her husband Leonard; Maynard Keynes, the economist; historian Lytton Stachey; and other writers including Yeats, Forster and Eliot. All were established in squares surrounding the British Museum.

THAT MAY BE the quickest summary of English literature you have ever read, but I wanted to give you just a taste of this rich stew called English literature and a desire to read more before we set out on our pilgrimage to literary London.

When I first wrote about this area, I described it as a bit solitary, abandoned and in disrepair. That is no longer an accurate description. There may have been more changes in this single, relatively small area, than any other place in London.

In the past few years, a new Globe Theatre has been erected near the location of the old one; a Clink Prison Museum has been developed where once only a small plaque identified the location; The *Golden Hinde*, a reconstruction of Sir France Drake's 16th century warship, has been anchored at the St. Mary Overie Dock and the whole area has been cleaned up and is swarming with visitors.

It is a particularly interesting part of Literary London and in addition has remarkable views of the north bank of London including stunning views of St. Paul's

Cathedral...a special gift for photographers.

DAY 1

Highlights: Southwark, Shakespeare Globe Museum, George Inn and the National Portrait Gallery.
Reservations: Check open hours at the Shakespeare Globe Museum. Telephone: 020-7902-1400
Tea at the Ritz Hotel. Telephone 020-493-8181. Reserve weeks in advance.
Dinner at Rules Restaurant. Telephone 020-836-5314
Theatre tickets for the Royal Shakespeare Company. Check newspapers for theatre times and productions.

IT SEEMS APPROPRIATE to begin your literary tour of London in **Southwark** on the south side of the Thames, near London Bridge. Chaucer's pilgrims met at the Tabard Inn on Southwark's High Borough Street and Shakespeare's Globe Theatre vied with the brothels and bear-baiting rings along the river.

Southwark was at the south end of the bridge the Romans first built across the river. It linked The City with this fishing village on the river's south side. Newer bridges provided the main connection from London through Southwark to the continent. The famous coaching inns along Borough High Street in Southwark supplied accommodations for Chaucer's pilgrims and other travelers.

Southwark later became an entertainment center with theaters, brothels and bear-baiting rings as well as the location of the Clink and Marshalsea Prisons. Mr. Micawber, in Dicken's David Copperfield, spent some time in Marshalsea prison when things did not turn up for him.

When the Thames froze, there were great frost fairs on the river. All this activity kept people amused as they waited for the morning opening of the bridge to take them into the city.

MORNING

① A T 9:30 A.M.: Take the tube to **London Bridge** tube stop, or cab to Borough High Street and the Southwark Cathedral.

If you tube, turn left as you leave the tube station and walk westward down London Bridge Street to **Borough High Street.** Cross the Borough High Street to **Bedale Street.** A quick right, diagonally across a parking lot, sometimes awash in cabbage leaves from the nearby vegetable market, will bring you to the **Southwark** ② **Cathedral.**

Wander through the Cathedral, noting especially the altar screen. The south wall bears a memorial sculpture of Shakespeare reclining and leaning on his left elbow. Above the sculpture is a stained glass window with figures from his plays. Nearby you will find a printed handout identifying the figures in the window.

It is not literary, but don't miss the Jacobean Tomb of Alderman Richard Humble (died 1616) and his wives along the side of the altar. Also note the very early wooden effigy of a knight, 1280-1300 and the brightly colored tomb of John Trehearne, 'gentleman porter' to James I. Be sure to visit the Harvard Chapel in honor of John Harvard, founder of our university and a member of this parish.

E XIT ON THE SOUTH PORCH and walk up the steps in front of you. Winchester Walk will be directly in front of you. Turn right immediately on **Cathedral Street.**

As you come around the corner, you will see St. Mary Overie Dock and *The Golden Hinde,* a full-size reconstruction of the 16th century warship in which Sir Francis Drake circumnavigated the world between 1577 and 1580.

It was built in Devon, England, and launched in 1973, when it completed its own circumnavigation of the world. Since then it has sailed to more than 300 ports worldwide, traveling over 140,000 miles. It is now permanently berthed here.

Five levels of decks can be explored, including the fourteen-cannon gun deck. The crew, dressed in 16th century costume, act as guides.

The ship is open 7 days a week, all year around, except Christmas Day. It is open from 10 a.m. to 6 p.m. in summer and from 10 a.m. to 5 p.m. in winter. Occasionally, the ship is closed during the day for educational and private functions. Call (0171) 403 0123 to confirm opening times on the day of your choice.

Admission is about $4 for adults; $2 for children and seniors. Tickets can be bought at a nearby shop which also sells nautical and gift items.

THE STREET CURVES around to the left where you will find the remains of an apparently unsupported standing wall with its original rose window, minus the stained glass. It is very strange to look up and see the blue sky and clouds through it.

This is all that remains of the **Winchester Palace**, the London residence from the 1140's to 1626 of the Bishop of Winchester. At that time, bishops were not only clergymen but great statesmen. From the river stairs at the end of Stoney Street, the Bishop could go by boat to the King's Court at Westminster. Most of the palace was destroyed by fire in 1814. What survived was built into warehouses; the west wall of the Great Hall with its 14th century Rose Window was saved.

You can still see the shape of the inner courtyard of the Palace next to this free-standing window.

Take the first right off Cathedral and you will be on **Clink Street**, the site of the infamous **Clink Prison** ⑨ and the source of our slang expression for going to jail.

As you walk along Clink Street, look for the Clink Street memorial plaque and the Clink Prison Museum, open 7 days a week, from 10 a.m. to 6 p.m.

As you walk, turn a bit toward your right and the river and you will find **Bankside**, which not surprisingly runs

along the river. During the Tudor reign, this area was outside the city's jurisdiction.

Here the famous theatres, such as the **Rose, Globe** and
Swan, thrived as well as the brothels, known as "stews"
with their fancy inmates known as Winchester geese. You
will look in vain for any traces of theatres or anything else
but here is where your imagination comes into play.

Just remember, this is where London grew and is
where Shakespeare and Chaucer once trod and worked.

As you walk along Bankside, you will arrive at the
③ **Anchor Pub**, built about 1775. Its exterior remains fairly
intact, although the interior has suffered some modern
renovation. There is a dining deck in front of the pub.

Walk across the deck and follow Bankside along the
river.

W ALK TO THE Southwark Bridge Road, turn left, and
continue to Park Street. Here stand the remains of
④ the original **Globe Playhouse** of Shakespeare's day.

The remains of the Globe consist of a plaque on a wall
on Park Street, close to the bridge: *Here stood the Globe
Playhouse of Shakespeare.* The Globe, built in 1599, used
timbers from the first playhouse in Shoreditch.

This first Globe Theatre burned down in 1613, when
cannon, fired during a performance of Shakespeare's
Henry VIII, set fire to the thatched roof. It was rebuilt and
existed until all playhouses were closed in 1642 by the
Puritans. It was demolished two years later.

After paying proper respects to this old site, turn right
and proceed to Bankside. A block or two to your left is the
amazing new **Globe Theatre and Exhibition.**

Due to the inspiration and determination of Sam
Wanamaker, American actor and director, the Globe was
reconstructed on a site on New Globe Walk near the
Thames and about two hundred meters from the original
theatre.

This amazing new/old building, a thatch-roofed, half-
timbered replica of the original open-air theatre, opened

in the spring of 1997 with Queen Elizabeth in attendance. A second theatre, the 300 seat Inigo Jones Theatre (named for the great British architect, has been built. Performances here take place year round.

Four plays are offered in the "big" Globe from June to September, performed in repertory during the day and evening. There is room for standees (the groundlings) and three galleries for other spectators.

Since tickets sell out early it is well to book in advance. Telephone bookings begin in early February. For reservations and credit card bookings call the Shakespeare Globe Box Office. 020/7401-9919.

For Postal bookings, send check or credit card details to: Shakespeare's Globe Box Office, New Globe Walk, Bankside, London SE1 9DT.

In addition to the theatre, the Globe includes an exhibition center with information about the theatre's history, construction and Shakespeare's works. Walking tours: Friday to Sunday every hour on the half hour 11:30 a.m. to 4:30 p.m., April through June; daily June through November.

Walk on down Bankside to **Cap Alley,** where you will find a plaque on a house facing the river that says Christopher Wren lived there. This is a private sign and probably not true. It was most likely a brothel, along with the other houses in the area. All these buildings are old and interesting.

Retrace your steps along Bankside, past the Cathedral and back to Borough High Street. Cross the High Street and visit a few of the old 'yards' or alleys along the street. King's Yard has nice facades and lamps; White Hart Yard is where Pickwick met Sam Weller in Dicken's novel and is now a parking spot.

The place you really want to see is the **George Yard Inn**, rebuilt in 1677. It houses the last galleried coaching inn in London.

NOON

⑦ **W**alk **into George Yard Inn's** courtyard to see the remaining two upper galleries. Dickens mentions this inn in "Little Dorrit." They still present plays in the courtyard during the summer, while in the winter, hot food is served in front of open fires.

The pub opens at 11:30 and lunch is served at noon. I recommend it for lunch. The pub lunch includes hot dishes, cold salads and pies - inexpensive and very good. You just sit at any table, joining the other eaters, which can be very pleasant.

AFTERNOON

SINCE YOU SPENT the morning on Chaucer and Shakespeare turf, I think it is now time to get an overview of the literary figures who graced England's history and there is no better place than at the **National Portrait Gallery.**

Take the London Bridge tube stop to Monument, where you change for either the circle or district line to Embankment tube stop. Walk up any of the streets north and you will arrive at **Trafalgar Square.** The portrait gallery is located directly behind the National Gallery. If this is too complicated, hail a cab on Borough High Street and cab to the museum.

Start on the top floor of the gallery. I will point out some of the special literary figures.

Room 1 has the great Chandos portrait of Shakespeare, the only known contemporary portrait of the playwright. The engravings for his First Folio are also displayed in this room. A miniature of Sir Walter Raleigh is in a display case with others.

Remember poor Walter languishing in the tower for 13 years because of something he wrote.

Room 3 has portraits of the diarist John Evelyn, the 79-year-old Isaac Walton, Dryden, Samuel Butler, and

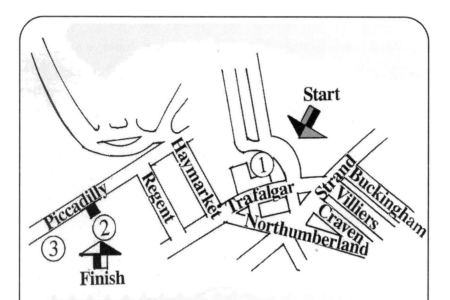

Start

Haymarket
Regent
Piccadilly
Trafalgar
Northumberland
Strand
Buckingham
Villiers
Craven

① ② ③

Finish

N

Literary London
Day 1
AFTERNOON

1/ National Portrait Gallery
2/ Fortnum & Mason
3/ Ritz Hotel

Regent's Park
British Museum
Camden Market
St. Paul's Cathedral
Canal Boat Landing
Tower of London
Buckingham Palace
Covent Garden
Hyde Park
Kensington Park
Westminster Abbey
Shake's Globe Theater
Southwark Cathedral
Victoria and Albert Museum
Harrod's
Parliament
Victoria Station
THAMES

Detail above

Milton. **Room 4** has the image of Samuel Pepys, which he mentions sitting for in his 1667 diary. In **Room 9** look for Dr. Johnson and his biographer, Boswell.

Room 13 is filled with representatives of the romantic movement: Scott, Lamb, Mary Shelley, Keats, Byron in a Greek outfit, Leigh Hunt, Wordsworth and Coleridge. The early Victorian literati are in **Room 17**: Tennyson, Dickens and Thackeray along with the remarkable portrait by Branwell Bronte of his three sisters. There is a ghostly shadow at the back of this painting, which some think was an image of Bran which he painted out. I like to imagine it is him looking over the shoulders of his more talented sisters.

The full-blown Victorian writers are in **Room 21**: Christina Rosetti and Ford Madox Brown. Here you will also find the Brownings, George Eliot, and Swinburne. And at last some photographs. These are by the great photographer, Julia Margaret Cameron, and include Tennyson and Carlyle. Lewis Carroll has taken his own portrait as well as one of Rossetti.

Room 24 has the Edwardian artists: Hardy, Irving, Kipling, Shaw and Oscar Wilde's caricature. T.E. Lawrence is on the mezzanine with photographs of Sassoon, Owen and Brooke.

On the **main floor**, sharing space with the royals, are James Joyce, W. H. Auden, Dylan Thomas and Vanessa Bell.

If you want to keep some of these images, the museum shop has black and white photographs of every item in the collection. Remarkable!

It is probably 3 or 3:30 p.m. by now. Walk down to Trafalgar and cross the Square, turn up the Strand to your left.

About one block along you will come to **Craven Street** on your right. Benjamin Franklin lived at 36 Craven St when he was the London agent to the General Assembly of Pennsylvania from 1757-75.

The block beyond is where you will find Rudyard Kipling's dwelling at **43 Villiers Street.** It was here that he wrote the *Barrack Room Ballads* and *The Light That Failed.*

And another block further on is Buckingham Street where you will find the home of the famous diary writer Pepys at number 12.

TEA TIME

WALK BACK to Trafalgar, cross the square, turn right up Haymarket til you come to **Piccadilly Circus.** Walk down Piccadilly to **Fortnum and Mason's** ② for sweets or a sandwich, or if you are feeling very elegant and have made a reservation, continue down Piccadilly to the **Ritz Hotel** for one of the fanciest teas in ③ London.

EVENING

SINCE THIS IS literary London, I suggest the theatre tonight. Go back to your hotel and rest an hour or so. The tea should hold you until supper after the theatre.

Since you walked in the shadows of the old Globe Theatre today, the **Royal Shakespeare Company** should do quite nicely this evening.

You might want to try supper at **Rules**, 35 Maiden Lane, after the performance. Just remember they do not take orders after 10 p.m.

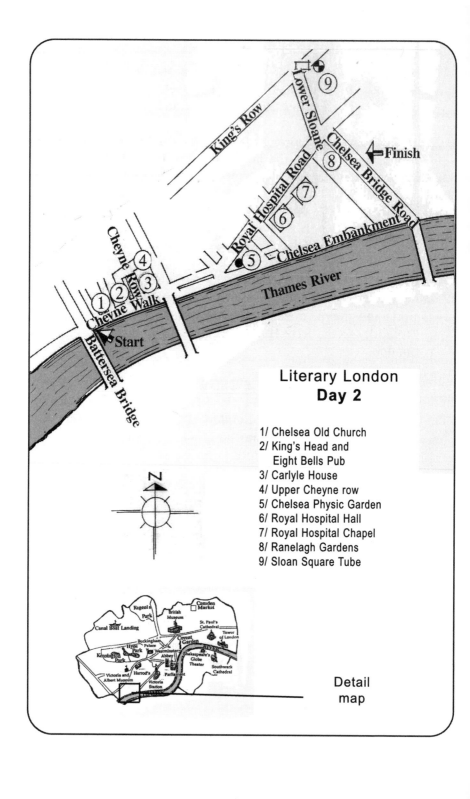

Literary London
Day 2

1/ Chelsea Old Church
2/ King's Head and
   Eight Bells Pub
3/ Carlyle House
4/ Upper Cheyne row
5/ Chelsea Physic Garden
6/ Royal Hospital Hall
7/ Royal Hospital Chapel
8/ Ranelagh Gardens
9/ Sloan Square Tube

Detail
map

DAY 2

Highlights: Westminster Abbey, Chelsea, Carlyle's House, Cheyne Walk, and the Barbican Center.
Reservations: Lunch at the King's Head & Eight Bells. Telephone 020-352-1820.
Theatre reservations at the Barbican Theatre. Check newspapers for productions and ticket information. Telephone 020-638-8891.

MORNING

TODAY START at **Westminster Abbey** at about 9 or 9:30 a.m. Remember: admission is now charged to enter the Abbey. You will want to look at everything, but particularly the Poet's Corner and some of the great memorials to literary figures in the abbey.

As you move down the North Aisle, look for the small wall plaque in the floor in the fourth bay. It is the memorial to playwright Ben Jonson with the famous misspelling, O rare Ben Johnson. Can you imagine making it into the abbey and then having them not spell your name right? Look also for the fine sculpture of Isaac Newton at this end of the north nave, just inside the altar rail.

Continue to make your way around the abbey. (Refer to the map and walk in *Basic Three Days in London*.) Work your way around to the south side of the abbey to the **Poets' Corner** and browse to your heart's delight.

I will mention just a couple of memorials to especially look for: the great one of Chaucer, the not- so-great one of Shakespeare, the burial stones of Dickens and Kipling and the memorials to W.H. Auden, Lewis Carroll and Dylan Thomas. This is one of those places to just look to your heart's content.

As you leave the abbey, check out their shop. They have a very nice stock of books and cards.

TAKE A CAB to **Chelsea.** If there is a line waiting for a cab, just go to the end and wait your turn. I jumped a line here one day and have never forgotten it.

You are going to spend the rest of the morning in Chelsea, home of the great Carlyle and many other noted literary figures.

I suggest a cab because there is not any kind of a decent tube ride to this part of London. The closest tube stop is at South Kensington or Sloane Square, blocks from where you want to go. Have the cabbie let you off at **Battersea Bridge** and **Cheyne Walk**, the street along the river. Battersea is the ugly iron bridge which took the place of the wooden bridge you remember seeing in paintings by Whistler and Turner. Walk east on Cheyne Walk past the Lindsey House, the original site of Thomas More's farm.

① THE **Chelsea Old Church** is on a site where a church has probably been located since Christianity came to England. In 1528 Sir Thomas More rebuilt the south chapel as his private chapel. During World War II bombing, the church was extensively damaged but has been restored. Note the chained books, including a Vinegar Bible (1717).

The pulpit is a copy of a original three decker ship. The monument to Sir Thomas More is in the Sanctuary against the south wall. Notice the embroidered kneelers begun in 1953, each commemorating a worshipper in the church or someone connected with it. Outside the church is a handsome sculpture of Sir Thomas More, which was unveiled in 1969.

NOON

② YOU SHOULD BE at the corner of Cheyne Walk and Cheyne Row at the inn called **King's Head & Eight Bells** (50 Cheyne Walk) where you have made your reservation for lunch.

This is actually two inns. You can eat and drink in a garden overlooking the Thames or in an upstairs restaurant. There is also a snack bar on the ground floor. The food is excellent and not expensive.

AFTERNOON

IT IS PROBABLY now about 1 or 1:30 p.m. Walk up Cheyne Row to **Thomas Carlyle's House,** number 24. Open ③ April to the end of October, open Wednesday to Sunday 11 a.m. to 5 p.m.

The house has been kept as it was in Carlyle's time. You will find portraits, furniture and letters from the Sage of Chelsea. Visit the top floor attic study with its skylight and the kitchen in the basement where Carlyle and Tennyson used to smoke. Here Carlyle wrote his famous books: The French Revolution, Heroes and Hero Worship, Frederick the Great and Past and Present.

Walk to **Upper Cheyne Row,** turn right to number 22, ④ Leigh Hunt's house, where he lived with his wife and 7 children and was visited by Shelley, Byron and Lamb. Walk back down Cheyne Row to Cheyne Walk and turn left. All those Cheynes are confusing, aren't they?

WALK ALONG the river and look at the houses. Look for a plaque marking the former location of Henry VIII's manor house. Number 16, the Queen's House, was the home of D. G. Rossetti, the pre-Raphaelite poet and the poet Swinburne. Rosetti kept an exotic menagerie in his garden including a wombat, armadillo, kangaroo, peacocks and a Brahmin bull with eyes like his wife, Janey, so he said. Note number 6 with its Chippendale-Chinese railings and gate and the red entrance to number 4 where George Eliot (Mary Ann Evans) died in 1880 after a residence of less than three weeks.

It will be mid afternoon by now. You should be passing the **Chelsea Physic Garden.** It is open mid-April to ⑤ mid-October, on Wednesday and Sunday, from noon to 5 p.m. and Sunday from 2 to 6 p.m. If you happen to be there on one of those days, stop in to see this wonderful garden founded in 1673 by the society of Apothecaries in London.

A nice amenity at the gardens, is **The Tearoom**, open only Wednesdays 2 to 5 p.m. and Sundays 2 to 6 p.m. Closed late November through March.

On the only two days the garden is open, its tearoom serves tea and cake for about $5. It is served in a rather ordinary Edwardian building, but you can carry your cakes and tea outside into the garden. This is all so British it makes me think I have discovered an insider's secret. Tea in the Chelsea Physic Garden, an eventuality devoutly to be hoped for.

We have come to the end of our literary tour for the day, but since you are in the area, and if you have the time, walk up to the **Royal Hospital** with its Wren buildings. You will see the Chelsea Pensioners (veterans) hospital, grounds open 10 a.m. to 8 p.m. **The chapel** and great hall are open daily 10 a.m. to noon and 2-4 p.m. Sunday 2-4 p.m.

And if you should be so lucky as to be there in May you might see the Chelsea Flower Show, one of London's great extravaganzas.

If not, walk through the adjacent **Ranelagh Gardens.** Take the Chelsea Bridge Road/Lower Sloane Street to **Sloane Square** and the tube stop. There are a number of lovely little shops on the square as well as the modern department store, Peter Jones.

EVENING

B ACK TO YOUR HOTEL for a rest and then the theatre again. Try the **Barbican Center** tonight.

You can take the tube to the Barbican stop where your walk to the center is very well signed and marked. In fact there is a yellow line painted on the walkways, which you follow right to the center. Just like the yellow brick road.

The center is a modern building in the middle of this old city, but I liked its layout and the theatres have wonderful sight lines and comfortable seats. Wander around the lobbies to see the exhibitions and listen to the performance of the informal music groups. I was happily surprised by the ambience of the place and how easy it was to get around. Enjoy.

DAY 3

Highlights: The Dickens House; Tavistock, Gordon, Russell and Bedford Squares; the British Library, Charing Cross Road and the bookstores.
Reservations: Dinner at the Ivy Restaurant, West Street.
Telephone 020-836-4751.

MORNING

TODAY YOU WILL visit **Bloomsbury,** a part of London which is a geographical location as well as a state of mind. I am sure everyone has a different thought when they hear the word, Bloomsbury.

To some it is the home of the British Museum, to others the location of London University, and to many the bailiwick of Virginia Woolf and her friends. It is all of those and more.

Its geographical boundary on the east, Gray's Inn Road, even encompasses the Dickens' House, the only remaining place where he lived in London.

Today you will start with Dickens and wander the great squares where Virginia and her compatriots lived.

THE **Dickens House**, 48 Doughty Street, is midway between the Russell Square and **Chancery Lane** tube stops, and a bit of a walk from either of them.

Or, just take a cab from your hotel. The house is open Monday through Saturday, from 10 a.m. to 5 p.m.

②

①

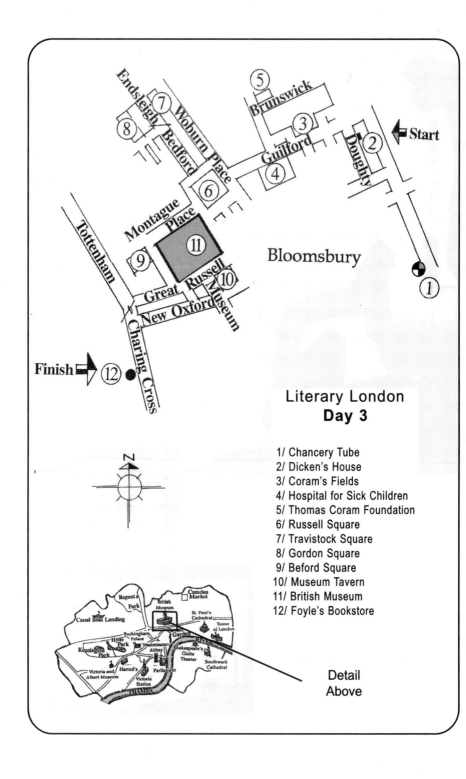

Bloomsbury

Start

Finish ⑫

N

Literary London
Day 3

1/ Chancery Tube
2/ Dicken's House
3/ Coram's Fields
4/ Hospital for Sick Children
5/ Thomas Coram Foundation
6/ Russell Square
7/ Travistock Square
8/ Gordon Square
9/ Beford Square
10/ Museum Tavern
11/ British Museum
12/ Foyle's Bookstore

Detail
Above

Dickens lived here from 1837-39, after his fame had became fairly secure, and wrote *Oliver Twist, Nicholas Nickleby* and *Barnaby Rudge.* You will see the desk on which he was working on the unfinished manuscript for *The Mystery of Edwin Drood* the day before he died. (Broadway produced a play suggesting a variety of endings to this story.)

The house is full of letters, manuscripts, portraits, furniture and relics as well as the most complete Dickens library in the world. Near where you buy your admission ticket is a case with a little portrait of Dickens and even a lock of his hair.

A FTER YOU LEAVE the house, walk up to Guilford Street, turn left and walk past **Coram's Fields**, a park for children. On your left you will see the **Foundation for Children** and behind it the **Hospital for Sick Children.**

Walk to **Russell Square** and turn right up Woburn Place to **Tavistock Square** and the adjoining **Gordon Square.** You are now in the **Bloomsbury** of the 20th century artists, writers and men and women of letters. About 1905, men from Cambridge began moving into this area; it was far enough from elegant Kensington to provide a break with that past and fresh air for new ideas.

Number 46 Gordon Square was the focus for much of this activity. The four children of Sir Leslie Stephen set up house there; Virginia Woolf was one of those young people. Later Maynard Keynes, the economist, held court here with his neighbors. Vanessa and Clive Bell lived at 50 Gordon Square, Lytton Strachey at 51 Gordon Square, Leonard and Virginia Woolf at 52 Tavistock Square.

Wander around these squares and try to imagine what it was like when the friendships which held these people together were translated into their salons, summer tennis games, attendance at new ballets by Diaghilev and the production of the twentieth century literature which changed our ideas.

Walk back to Russell Square and on to Montague

⑨ Place and **Bedford Square**, the best preserved of all of these great squares with its three story brick houses. Bedford is along the west side of the British Museum.

NOON

⑩
⑪ **W**alk to Great Russell Street, turn left and just opposite the **British Museum** at the corner of Great Russell and Museum Streets you will find the **Museum Tavern**. It is now time for lunch and this is a fine place for a shepherd's pie or salad.

AFTERNOON

THIS AFTERNOON you will visit one of London's newest treasures, the **British Library.** Once housed in the British Museum, across from the pub you just visited, it is now up near St. Pancras Station at 96 Euston Road. Free admission, Open Monday to Saturday, 10 a.m. to 5 p.m.; Sunday 2:30 to 6 p.m. Call to make sure of admission: (0171) 412 7000. Take a cab since it is not an easy tube connection and it is a relatively short distance.

Hopefully, you will be able to see King John's *Magna Carta* (1215), the *Gutenberg Bible*, Captain Cook's journals, manuscripts by Dickens, Keats, Lewis Carroll, Charlotte Bronte, et al. Check out the Shakespeare memorabilia, including a mortgage with his signature and the *First Folio* of 1623.

If you still have time left this afternoon, cab back to
⑫ Charing Cross Road where you can visit **Foyle's** famous bookstore and many others along this street of books.

EVENING

DINNER TIME. And theatre if you wish. A final suggestion. Walk down Charing Cross Road to the Cambridge Circus. To the east of the Circus, on your left as you walk south on Charing Cross, you will find little

West Street and **The Ivy Restaurant.** Directly across the street is St. Martin's Theatre where Agatha Christie's *The Mousetrap* has been playing since 1952. From the sublime of Bloomsbury to the ridiculous of *The Mousetrap* might be just what you need tonight.

And The Ivy is sublime. It is one of my favorite dining places in London because it is so British and the management is so welcoming.

MORE TOURS

A S YOU CAN GUESS, despite three days of retracing London's literary heritage, you have just put a sizeable dent in it.

One very special place and a bit out of the way is **Keats House** in **Hampstead**, open January to October, Tuesday to Sunday 12 to 5 p.m.; November to December, noon to 4 p.m.

Keats wrote the *Ode to a Nightingale* in this garden and became engaged to Fanny Brawne, who lived in the other half of this semi-detached house. It was here he became ill with tuberculosis in 1820 and from here he left for Rome to spend the winter in an apartment overlooking the Spanish Steps, where he died in 1821.

You could walk up **Wimpole Street** to see the place from which Elizabeth Barrett left to marry Robert Browning, although the house is no longer there.

Baker Street still holds the ghost of Sherlock Holmes and his friend, Watson.

And **Madame Tussaud's waxworks** still features Agatha Christie, comfortably ensconced in a chair with a pillow at her back, and Hans Christian Andersen preparing to read his rather odd tales to children.

O NE OF THE BEST THINGS about London is that you never run out of new discoveries, old friends or exciting adventures. No wonder so many writers have lived in and loved this city.

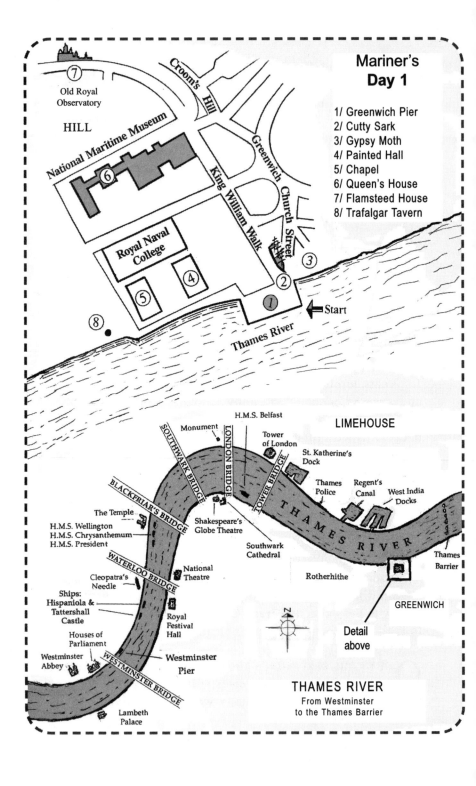

Mariner's
Day 1

1/ Greenwich Pier
2/ Cutty Sark
3/ Gypsy Moth
4/ Painted Hall
5/ Chapel
6/ Queen's House
7/ Flamsteed House
8/ Trafalgar Tavern

Old Royal Observatory

HILL

National Maritime Museum

Croom's Hill

Greenwich Church Street

King William Walk

Royal Naval College

Start

Thames River

Monument

H.M.S. Belfast

LIMEHOUSE

SOUTHWARK BRIDGE

LONDON BRIDGE

Tower of London

St. Katherine's Dock

BLACKFRIAR'S BRIDGE

TOWER BRIDGE

Thames Police

Regent's Canal

West India Docks

The Temple

Shakespeare's Globe Theatre

THAMES RIVER

H.M.S. Wellington
H.M.S. Chrysanthemum
H.M.S. President

Southwark Cathedral

Thames Barrier

WATERLOO BRIDGE

National Theatre

Rotherhithe

Cleopatra's Needle

Ships:
Hispaniola &
Tattershall
Castle

Royal Festival Hall

GREENWICH

Houses of Parliament

N

Westminster Abbey

WESTMINSTER BRIDGE

Westminster Pier

Detail above

Lambeth Palace

THAMES RIVER
From Westminster
to the Thames Barrier

MARINER"S
LONDON

You don't have to be a sailor
to enjoy this nautical outing

MOST PEOPLE don't think of boating when they think of London, yet it is Britain's love of the sea that built the empire. London grew from the Thames River; the river was this wonderful city's first thoroughfare and its major entry to the ocean. The river was London's processional parade ground and the site for funeral processions for such illustrious folks as Elizabeth I and Winston Churchill.

As early as 60 A.D., after the Romans had defeated the Celts, London was a busy port. In 836 the Vikings sailed up the Thames to sack the city. In 1014, the Anglo-Saxons stormed London, tied their boats to the pilings of London Bridge and sailed down the river, pulling the bridge down behind them. Remember the song, *London Bridge Is Falling Down?* It really did fall down. During the Middle Ages, London was the only international port in Britain.

In the 19th century, the East and West India trading companies began constructing docks for their sugar, grain, bananas and hard wood. Eventually there were 665 acres of dock basins and 36 miles of piers. Thousands of ships sailed the river and anchored at its ports. Following World War II, the bulk of the port activity moved to Tilbury and most of the docks became empty and dark.

Today development projects along the river are underway at St. Katherine's Docks, adjacent to the Tower of London, and at the incredible Docklands on the Isle of Dogs.

D URING THIS special three-day tour of London, you will see boats galore, from sailing barges to the most famous sailing ship of them all, the *Cutty Sark*. You'll take a quiet cruise up the historic Thames, see a three-decker pulpit, retrace some of the glories of sailing through the National Maritime Museum and eat aboard a restaurant ship. You will see a recreation of Lord Nelson's battle on the *H.M.S. Victory*, visit a 7th century royal burial ship, and boat through London's canal system.

A few notes. Double check the times for boat sailings. Greenwich tourist information: 020 7930-4097. Dates and times of sailings are subject to change. Remember: the temperature on the water is usually at least ten degrees cooler than on land, so dress accordingly. A scarf or a cap can be particularly welcome on windy days. Binoculars are also very useful for spotting sights along the shore.

DAY 1

Highlights: Greenwich, The National Maritime Museum, Queen's House, the Cutty Sark and Gypsy Moth, Royal Naval College, Observatory and Docklands.

Reservations: Hispaniola restaurant ship. Telephone 020 7839-3011.

MORNING

S TART YOUR TOUR at **Westminster Pier** about 10 a.m. Westminster tube stop is located near the pier on the Thames River.

Today you will be spending the day at **Greenwich**, a

sailor's paradise, with its sailing ships, naval museum and college, and old seafaring pubs.

Walk over to the pier. The **Houses of Parliament, Big Ben** and **Westminster Abbey** are looming over your shoulder.

The river launches operate from April to October. The boats to Greenwich run approximately every 30 minutes, 10:30 a.m. to 4 p.m. The trip will take about 45 minutes.

As you travel east on the river you will see the **Victoria Embankment** on your left. At the footbridge, notice the *Hispaniola,* a restaurant boat on your left. The National Theatre complex is on your right.

Moored along the embankment you will see the *Wellington,* a World War II frigate now serving as livery hall of the Honorable Company of Master Marines, and the *Chrysanthemum* and *President,* World War I sloops, now training ships of the London Division of the Royal Naval Volunteer Reserve. You will pass under the Blackfriars, Southwark and London bridges, plus the two new bridges, the Hungerford and the Millennium bridges.

Soon you will see, on your right, the *H.M.S. Belfast,* which you will visit tomorrow, and on your left, the **Tower of London,** with the 19th-century **Tower Bridge** directly in front of you. Its 1100-ton arms can be raised in an astonishing three minutes to allow tall masted ships to pass.

As you travel up the river, you will see the St. Katherine Docks. Note the **Execution Dock** marked with the letter E. Here is where Captain Kidd and other pirates were hung and their bodies left to permit the tide waters to 'wash over them three times'.

You can see the Prospect of Whitby, an old pub, and miles of wine vaults under the London Dock warehouses. The towns of Wapping and Rotherhite are on your right. Rotherhite was where the Pilgrim's *Mayflower* was built. The Mayflower's captain was buried in Rotherhite's St. Mary's church yard when he returned in 1621.

The Surrey Commercial Docks with their uncertain future are now on your right and the sweeping peninsula called the Isle of Dogs on your left. This is now the incredible **Docklands** you will visit later today.

① **Y**OU ARE NOW at the pier at **Greenwich**. Greenwich is the home of the Flamsteed House, former home of the Royal Observatory; the Royal Naval College; the National Maritime Museum and its connecting Queen's House, from which our White House was designed.

The Greenwich Tourist Information Center is open daily from 10 .m. to 5 p.m. They provide walking tours as well as general information.

But the first sight you see will be the masts of the clip-
② per ship *Cutty Sark* in dry dock at the pier. When she was launched in 1869 she was the fastest clipper afloat, posting 363 miles per day during her China tea trade days. Open every day, all year round from 10 a.m. to 5 p.m.

Be sure to go on deck as well as down into her hold to see the collection of carved wooden figureheads from old ships.

③ Next to her is the small ketch, the *Gipsy Moth IV,* on which Sir Francis Chichester circumnavigated the world alone in 1966-67. Chichester's trip covered 29,677 miles over the space of 226 days. You can visit her during the same hours as the *Cutty Sark.*

The domed building next to the river is the entrance to a foot tunnel which goes underneath the Thames River. You will find 100 steps and an elevator which will take you to a foot tunnel underneath the Thames to the Isle of Dogs. It is about a 10 minute walk to the other side where you will see the magnificent view of Greenwich which Canaletto painted.

NOON

⑧ **T**HE HISTORIC **Trafalgar Tavern**, on the waterfront near the Royal Chapel, built in 1837, was described by

Dickens in *Our Mutual Friend*, a novel set near the Thames.

An old Victorian pub, the **Rose and Crown**, is at 1 Crooms Hill, near the observatory; the **Gypsy Moth** is at 60 Greenwich Church St.

There are also a number of tearooms scattered about for mid-afternoon sustenance.

AFTERNOON

WALK UP King William Walk to the **National Maritime Museum**, the Old Royal Observatory and the Queen's House, open daily 10 a.m. to 5 p.m. The Queen's House contains 16th and 17th century models of ships, maps, navigational instruments and paintings. ⑥

The Maritime Museum is the greatest seafaring museum in the world and is contained in two wings on either side of the Queen's House. The **East Wing** contains 19th and 20th century model ships and other materials pertaining to the Royal Navy. Don't miss the navigation room with its naval instruments or the collection of Nelson memorabilia.

The **Neptune Hall** in the West Wing exhibits full size boats such as a 1907 paddle tug, the *Reliant*; riverboats and Prince Frederick's 1732 barge. This is a sailor's paradise.

WHEN YOU can bear to leave this treasure house, visit **Flamsteed House**, formerly the Royal Observatory. The observatory was moved to Herstmonceux in Sussex in 1948-49 because of the growing pollution of Greenwich's atmosphere. ⑦

The Flamsteed House, designed by Sir Christopher Wren, is now an annex of the maritime museum and contains a fine collection of astronomy and navigation instruments. The Caird Planetarium is nearby. They are at the top of a hill surrounded by Greenwich Park, a long, steep walk. These buildings are open daily 10 a.m. to 5 p.m.

The famous **zero meridian of longitude** passes through the House. However Greenwich no longer sets the world's clocks. The chronometers, long out of date, were replaced in 1985 by cesium atoms in a bureau of weights and measures in downtown Paris. For most of us, time still belongs to Greenwich.

Mariners will be fascinated with the old marine time-keepers, refracting telescope, celestial globes, quadrants, sextants and chronometers. Incidentally the second Astronomer Royal from 1720 to 1742 was a man by the name of Edmond Halley, after whom the comet is named.

WALK BACK DOWN THE HILL and turn right to the **Royal Naval College,** open daily ten to 5 p.m. Christopher Wren, the architect for St. Paul's Cathedral, was also the architect for the College.

The refectory and chapel are matching buildings, placed just opposite each other. The refectory contains the amazing **Painted Hall,** a Baroque masterpiece by Sir James Thornhill. When I was there, the dining room was set for a ceremonial banquet with great silver pieces and tiny pink silk shaded lights on the long tables. This is an extraordinary room.

Walk across the open green space to the **Chapel,** which is designed in a much lighter style. Notice the altar-piece by Benjamin West and the round pulpit made by Lawrence to look like the top deck of a three-decker ship.

WALK BACK TO THE RIVER and the **foot tunnel**, located near the *Cutty Sark.* A ten-minute walk will take you across (underneath) the Thames River to **Docklands.** Once the busiest port in the world, today its 55 miles of waterfront provide a backdrop for the world's largest urban renewal program.

Docklands covers an area larger than the city of London and West End combined. This is a new city in the making. It includes Canary Wharf with its complex of offices, restaurants, shops and markets. Cesar Pelli's tower looms over this area. Nearby West India Quay and Billingsgate Fish Market can be viewed across the West India Dock. Many buildings on this peninsula have been restored and there is spectacular contemporary architecture, landscapes, bridges and waterscapes.

When you exit the footbridge (there is an elevator to take you to the top), walk over to the river to see the wonderful view of Greenwich, which you just left. This is a photographer's dream of a view.

The tip of Docklands where you find yourself contains a small town, Cubitt Town; a lovely little old church, Christ and St. John with Saint Luke, a ten-minute walk away and Mudchute, Europe's largest urban farm.

At this southern limit of the Isle of Dogs you will find the last stop on this route of **Docklands Light Railway** (DLR), the London's newest automatic elevated railway. All Travelcards are valid on this railway. You can take this railway to either the Bank or Tower Hill tube stop or return to Central London.

You could get off at the Crossharbour stop to see the Visitor Center or continue to Canary Wharf to see the Pelli Tower and the surrounding development.

As you train across this remarkable terrain be sure to look for the Millennium Dome just west of the south Quay stop, to the West. It is hard to miss. No one is quite sure what is going to happen inside this enormous dome.

The ride back on the DLR is remarkable: wonderful views of this incredible building operation, ships, Limehouse, Westferry, Shadwell and the old pubs along the river.

Too soon you are back in Central London.

EVENING

Dinner on the **Hispaniola** can be very pleasant at night. Dinner will cost between $30 and $40. Or you can just have a pleasant drink on the topdeck of the ship.

Tomorrow you will be off to Tower Pier and a visit to the historic St. Katherine's Docks, the H.M.S. Belfast and a historic sailor's pub.

DAY 2

Highlights: Trafalgar Square, H.M.S. Belfast and St. Katherine's Docks
Reservations: Dickens Inn for dinner. Telephone 020 7488 2208.

MORNING

START THE DAY at about 8:30 or 9 a.m. at **Trafalgar Square.** No matter the intentions of Charles I or architect John Nash to design this space for other purposes, it is clearly now the place which honors naval power and its glory.

Admiral Lord Nelson, England's greatest naval hero, is honored by the 150-foot column in memory of his victory over the French fleet at Trafalgar in 1805. As you remember, Nelson died on the deck of his ship, the *H.M.S. Victory*, just as the battle had been won. Admirals Beatty and Jellicoe were commemorated with statues in 1949 at the same time the fountains were installed. Edwin Landseer's four lions at the base of the column were cast in 1868 from cannon recovered from the ship, the *Royal George*, which sank in Portsmouth harbor in 1782 with hundreds of casualties. The two huge round lamps on the square are from Nelson's flagship, the *Victory*.

Proceed up **Whitehall.** The Admiralty Arch will be on your right; it honors Queen Victoria. The first large building on your right is the **Admiralty**, governing body of the Royal Navy. It is open by appointment only.

Continue up Whitehall past the **Banqueting Hall,** the **Horse Guards, Number 10 Downing Street,** the **Cenotaph of 1919**, memorial to Britain's war dead and on to **Westminster Abbey, Parliament** and **Big Ben.**

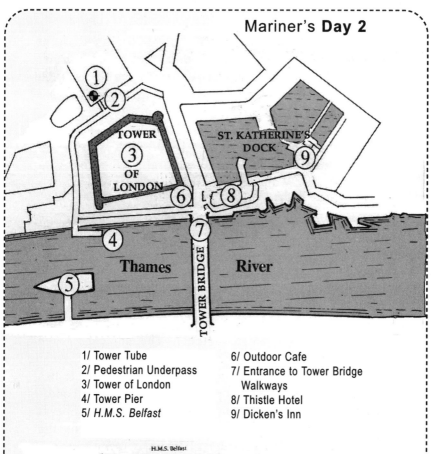

Mariner's **Day 2**

1/ Tower Tube
2/ Pedestrian Underpass
3/ Tower of London
4/ Tower Pier
5/ *H.M.S. Belfast*

6/ Outdoor Cafe
7/ Entrance to Tower Bridge
   Walkways
8/ Thistle Hotel
9/ Dicken's Inn

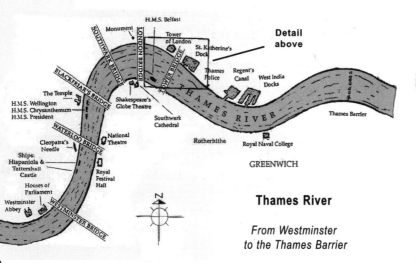

Thames River

*From Westminster
to the Thames Barrier*

① AT THIS POINT you can choose to boat from Westminster pier to Tower pier, part of the journey you took yesterday, or you can take the Westminster tube stop to Tower Hill station. In either event you will arrive at the **Tower of London** from where you will visit a historic mariner's area.

② If you rode the Tube, take the **pedestrian subway** to cross underneath the busy street separating the tube stop from the Tower. Walk toward the Tower, following the
③ signs to **Tower Pier.**

④ From the pier, a **launch** will take you across the Thames to Symons Wharf where the *H.M.S. Belfast* is docked. This World War II warship (Southhampton class cruiser) took part in the Normandy landings, the Battle of North Cape in 1943, the Arctic convoys and finally the Korean war. You can visit the *Belfast* from 10 a.m. to 5 p.m from November through February; and from 10 a.m. to 6 p.m., March through October. The launches leave every 20 minutes.

You will be able to wander all over the ship. It has been preserved as closely as possible to its original condition. Areas open to the public are the messdecks, operations room, sick bay, boiler room, engine room, and the captain's and admiral's bridges.In addition you can see the punishment cells, and two of the four 6-inch gun turrets.

A complete tour of the vessel will take about two hours. A shop provides wallcharts, postcards and other souvenirs. Be warned: some of the ship's ladders are quite steep.

Return to **Tower Pier** by launch. Walk up the stairs from the pier, turn right and walk along the river in front of the Tower to **St. Katherine Docks,** where you will spend the afternoon.

You will pass the Tower's **famous cannons** and see a remarkable view of the river with its continuous parade of shipping.

NOON

THERE ARE PLEASANT **outdoor cafes** along this walkway ⑥
which I recommend for lunch.

AFTERNOON

AFTER LUNCH walk up a flight of steps to **Tower** ⑦
Bridge, built in 1886-94. The 800-foot-long span
includes twin drawbridges, each weighing almost 1,000
tons. They can be raised in a minute and a half to permit
the passage of large vessels.

Visit the twin towers and museum; enjoy the panoramic views of the river and the city from the glass enclosed
walkways 140 feet above the river. The towers are open
from 10 a.m. to 6:30 p.m. Walk out a short distance on the
bridge to the ticket booths and the elevator or steps which
will take you to the walkways. Level 3 features an exhibition of the structural and hydraulic engineering of the
bridge with video film, drawings and photographs showing how it works. Level 4 is the location for the two glass-
enclosed walkways. Special sliding windows make it possible for photographers to obtain fine views.

The **South Tower** holds an exhibition of the history of
the City's bridges. The Museum contains the original boil-
ers and engines which powered the bridge prior to electri-
fication. There is also a shop with publications and postcards.

You will now visit **St. Katherine's Dock** area, badly
damaged during World War II and abandoned until about
1968, now containing a yacht basin with about 200 yachts.
Visitors can become temporary members of the yacht club
on application. Wander around the marina to see the
unusual assortment of boats moored to the piers.

Back down the bridge steps, cross the street and walk
past the **Tower Thistle Hotel.** Walk in front of the hotel ⑧
on the river side to see the plantings, sculptures and river.

Pass a marina on your left, and you will come to the **Dickens Inn** directly in front of you. The collection of old ships has been moved.

Continue walking along the Thames to explore the tremendous new **Dockside** development. New buildings, docks, promenades, restaurants, and dockages are being built at a rapid rate. The process is well underway, but far from complete.

EVENING

WALK AROUND the dock area to see the marinas with the anchored yachts; soon it will be time for dinner. Nearby **Dickens Inn** includes an ale bar with snacks, which is inexpensive, and the more costly restaurant.

Or, you can cab over to the famous pub, the **Prospect of Whitby**, where Whistler and Turner painted and mariners gathered. Tomorrow you leave the river and turn inland to London's historic canals.

DAY 3

Highlights: Regent's Canal and Park, Madame Tussaud's Wax Museum, and the British Museum.

Reservations: Canal boat passage. The London Waterbus Company. Telephone 020 7482-2660 or 2550. Canal boat with lunch. Jason's Trip. Telephone 020 7286-3428. Jenny Wren. Telephone 020 7485-4433 or 485-6210.

MORNING

TODAY YOU WILL ride a canal boat, "experience" the Battle of Trafalgar, visit a burial ship and end your three-day visit to London's marine treasures by floating down the river to enjoy the illuminated city.

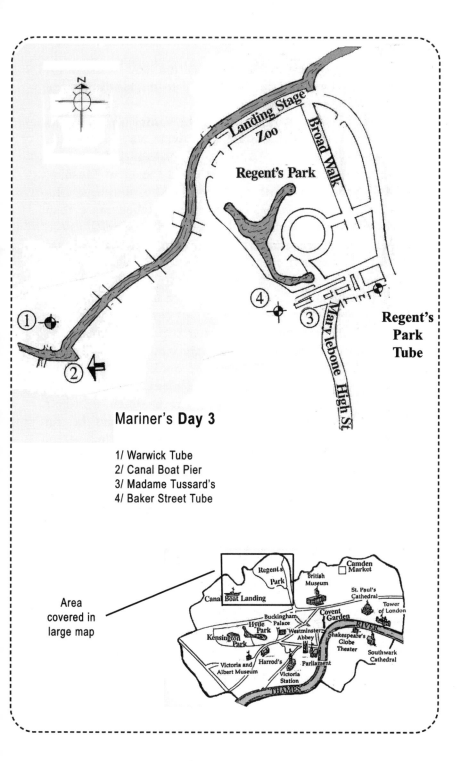

N

Landing Stage

Zoo

Broad Walk

Regent's Park

④

③

Marylebone High St.

①

②

Regent's
Park
Tube

Mariner's **Day 3**

1/ Warwick Tube
2/ Canal Boat Pier
3/ Madame Tussard's
4/ Baker Street Tube

Area
covered in
large map

Regent's
Park

Camden
Market

British
Museum

St. Paul's
Cathedral

Canal Boat Landing

Tower
of London

Buckingham
Palace

Covent
Garden

Hyde
Park

Westminster
Abbey

Shakespeare's
Globe
Theater

Kensington
Park

RIVER

Southwark
Cathedral

Victoria and
Albert Museum

Harrod's

Parliament

Victoria
Station

THAMES

①   Tube to **Warwick Avenue** station and walk down Warwick Avenue to Blomfield Road to the **landing stage** or cab to the **canal boat pier.**

②   You are now at London's **Little Venice** and ready to explore its eight-and-one-half mile waterway, which cuts through the city along some of its landmarks: Regent's Park, London Zoo, Primrose Hill and the great Mosque. The canal was officially opened in 1820, joining a network of historic waterways which stretched more than 4,000 miles throughout England. It is still a special way to see this city. Three boat lines operate this part of the canal between Easter and mid-October.

    The **London Waterbus Company** shuttles between Little Venice and Camden Lock, with a landing at the zoo. **Jason's Trip** has a one and one half hour trip on a 1906 narrow boat, with lunch; a similar trip is offered by the **Jenny Wren.** Trips run approximately every hour from 10 a.m. to 4:30 p.m. It is necessary to book in advance. The canal is lined with houseboats and pleasure craft, which are enthusiastically decorated by the boatmen and their families. The choice is yours, but I'd recommend the trip to the landing at the **London Zoo.** The Waterbus offers this trip for about $8 to $10, including the admission fee to the zoo.

    When you leave the boat, you are at the far end of the zoo. Walk through this world famous animal garden, stopping to see the pandas from China and the great aviary. Cut through Regent's Park to Queen Mary's Gardens.

NOON

S TOP AT EITHER the **tea house** or **restaurant** for some sustenance.

AFTERNOON

W ALK OUT THE ENTRANCE and two blocks straight ahead to Marylebone Road. To your right is **Madame Tussaud's** wax museum. It is all quite remark- ③ able, but it is for their reconstruction of *The Battle of Trafalgar* that I now recommend it to you.

You enter the scene to the sound of bands playing *Heart of Oak* as they did for Nelson's fleet nearing the French and Spanish warships in October, 1805. The battle with its gunfire, smoke, dust, noise, and the dying Nelson, is quite astounding. At the last, you hear the sound of bells ringing for the dead, along with their victory toll, just as the church bells rang for the quick and the dead so long ago.

O NE LAST STOP TODAY: the **British Museum**. The tube connections are awkward, so walk back to Marylebone Road and hail a cab.

You will be particularly interested in the **Sutton Hoo Treasures** in Room 41. These objects came from a 7th century royal burial ship, excavated in Suffolk in 1939, the richest ever found in Europe. Included are gold and jewels, a wonderful helmet, shield and sword, drinking horns, bottles, bowls, bronze and iron utensils, metalwork and even textiles. It was an extraordinary find.

Walk out the main entrance and across Great Russell Street to the **Museum Tavern** which opened its doors in 1703. I love this old place...the wood paneling and cut glass windows; the nice people, the shepherd's pie and the bar with its lagers, wines, ales and cider.

EVENING

T ONIGHT TAKE one of the **Thames River supper cruis- es** from Westminster pier. These often include a basket supper and last an hour and a half.

Evening cruises from Westminster Pier usually are

available from 7:30 to 9:15 p.m. or 8:15 to 10 p.m. Check schedules since they are subject to change. This is a leisurely way to end your mariner's tour of London and a have a last glimpse of this magnificent lighted city from its main thoroughfare

EXTRA DAY TOUR

IF YOU HAVE AN EXTRA DAY, slip away to **Portsmouth**, England's old and historic seaport. It's about 70 miles to the southwest of London, an easy two hours by train or two hours, twenty minutes by bus.

In the **Portsmouth Naval Base** you'll find the marvelous *HMS Victory*, Lord Nelson's flagship, launched in 1765, and today a national treasure that is maintained as she appeared at the time of the battle of Trafalgar.

You can trod the decks where England's great sea lord paced and go below to get an idea of what life was like for the ordinary seaman. As you look about, try to imagine being part of an 850-man crew in the 226-foot-long hull.

For a special sense of history, go deep in the hull to the **orlop deck,** where they carried Lord Nelson after he was shot. Look about you; sniff the air. This is the original part of the ship.

Some of the aura of the days of the old wooden ships still remains. Walk about the ship, admiring the ancient hull.

WALK A SHORT DISTANCE to a modernistic structure that houses the special archeological treasure, the *Mary Rose.* This was King Henry VIII's flagship that tragically sank in 1545 not far from shore in full view of the king. She was recovered in 1982 after nearly four centuries under the sea and today as you enter a moisture-filled chamber you can see this very old, and very wet, ship.

There are some 20,000 items also on display recovered from the ancient ship and from her crew, nearly all of whom perished when she capsized.

A short distance away is the elegant frigate **H.M.S. Warrior**, England's first iron warship, built in 1860.

Walk through the **Royal Naval Museum**, where you can see all sorts of naval memorabilia.

A splendid day, all in all, on the coast of England overlooking the English Channel and the Isle of Wright, replete with wonderful ships and a special sense of history. *Bon Voyage.*

Shopping
Day 1

1/ Piccadilly Circus
2/ Liberty's
3/ Selfridge's
4/ Marks and Spencer
5/ Burlington arcade
6/ Fortnum & Mason
7/ Trafalgar Square
8/ Hispaniola

Area covered in large map

THAMES
RIVER
⑧ Finish

SHOPPER'S LONDON

Here's a tour through the best
of London's elegant, quaint, or just plain fun
places to shop. Bring money.

L ONDON IS one of the greatest shopping centers in the world. If you can't find it in
London it probably doesn't exist. London has
shops so elegant you have probably never heard
their names; it has the largest department store
in Europe and shops so tiny you can scarcely
wedge your way through the door.

Remember hearing that England is a country
of shopkeepers? It's *true.*

During this three-day tour, you will go to
some of the most famous and some not-so-
famous shopping streets, including Regent and
Bond Street, Charing Cross and Bond Street,
and Convent Garden, Knightsbridge and
Kensington.

I will throw in a fourth day for London markets, which are generally held on Friday,
Saturday or Sunday. If you happen to be in
London on one of those days, you may want to
visit the markets or substitute one of them for
one of the three days of shopping.

Just a few reminders and suggestions to help
make your shopping more pleasant:

Hours: Most shops are open from 9 a.m. to 5:30 p.m. Mondays through Saturdays. A few close Saturday afternoon.

On Wednesdays, shops in the Knightsbridge, Sloane Square and King's Road areas stay open until 7 p.m., and on Thursday, shops in the West End are open till 7:30 p.m. Convent Garden shops are open until 8 p.m., six days a week.

Shopping will be pleasanter and safer with travelers checks or credit cards. Although London is a very safe city, pickpockets work in crowded shopping streets. Remember to always get a receipt in case you want to exchange, receive credit or get a cash refund. You are entitled to ask for a cash refund in preference to a credit slip. All large shops will accept internationally recognized credit cards.

Value Added Tax (VAT): This is the scheme which enables overseas visitors to avoid paying the standard 17.5 percent sales tax on purchases to be taken out of the country. (See VAT advice in the earlier chapter on Practical Information).

Just a few suggestions: Some stores are able to send goods abroad free of the VAT. Otherwise you must ask for a VAT form at the time of purchase, fill it out and present it and the goods at VAT desks at the airport when you leave the country. You must then send the form back to the store to receive reimbursement. It is a complicated, unwieldy and often financially unsound system since you may lose money on the exchange procedures. Many shops have a minimum price below which goods cannot be purchased under this system.

My advice is that unless the purchase is substantial, forgo the tax relief.

DAY 1

Highlights: Regent and Bond Streets, St. James's Street, Oxford Street, and Burlington Arcade.

MORNING

Today you will visit the Regent and Bond Street areas and spend the afternoon in the St. James's enclave.

Start the day at **Piccadilly Circus.** Walk north on ①
Regent Street along the curved section known as the Quadrant.

John Nash designed the original Regent Street thoroughfare, which was intended to enable the royals to drive from Carlton House to their new Regent's Park. By the time the street was finished in 1823, the royal family had moved to Buckingham Palace; the avenue was never completed according to the original plan.

Walk north up the street, crossing back and forth to see the places that most interest you. You will notice that the cross streets change names from the right to the left of Regent Street, so it is difficult to give you the names of corners.

At the end of the first block at Glasshouse Street, on your right, is **Aquascutum**, the famous shop for raingear, and across the street is **Austin Reed** for the gentleman.

Two blocks beyond you will come to Beak Street on your right. As you go down Beak Street, one block off Regent and to your left, you will see **Carnaby Street**. During the swinging '60s, here is where the Beatles and Twiggy shopped and their followers followed.

Carnaby Street has bounced back after being virtually discarded. Many new and innovative shops have set up business here and on the surrounding streets.

Places are changing so rapidly you have to go see for yourself. Do check out **Mikey** at 25 Carnaby, for its huge selection of fashionable jewelry with moderate prices. But now you know that Carnaby Street is back.

Return to Regent Street and one of London's smartest shops, **Zara** at 118 Regent. This is part of 500 branches worldwide, but it is filled with reasonably priced versions of the seasons smartest clothing...especially good men's clothing. **Burberry's** at Number 165 is for raingear. Expensive, but superb. On your right is Gered's for china and the great goldsmiths, Mappin & Webb. Then you come to Hamleys for toys and games, an amazing place. You could play there for hours.

②   **Liberty & Company** is at the corner of Regent and Great Marlborough Streets. Its Renaissance building, with a neo-Tudor addition, is one of London's most fascinating stores.

This magnificent place is so filled with nooks and crannies that I almost always get temporarily lost. Their printed silks are world famous. Take some time to explore this most unusual store.

Proceed on Regent to find other fine department stores across from Liberty's: Dickins & Jones, Bally shoes, Laura Ashley, Godiva's and Crabtree and Evelyn.

If you turn east (to your right) on Oxford Street you will come to **Marks & Spencer**, one of London's oldest and most popular department stores. Across the street, look for Mango, three floors of a modern three story store filled with trendy and inexpensive clothing.

Just at the corner of Regent and Oxford is the ever-popular H & M. Lots of inexpensive children's clothes.

Turn left on Oxford and Regent Street and you will find your way to another of London's famous department stores, **Selfridges.** Its ground floor is cosmetic heaven; the third floor filled with lovely lingerie and in between gorgeous designer clothing. It also has a restaurant, a café and a beauty shop.

Go east on Oxford, for a few blocks to New Bond Street where you will find the great jeweler Asprey at number 167. Look for Nicole's at number 158 for stylish clothes and a very smart and popular restaurant in the "lower level"...basement to me.

Cartier, another fabulous jewellery store is at 175-76 and Mikimoto with its gorgeous pearls is at 179. Burberry, Ungaro, Donna Karan, Calvin Klein and Versace are all along this remarkable street.

Look for Chappell of Bond Street, established in 1811, has an enormous selection of printed music and musical instruments. Even the stationery store Smythsons is at Number 40 New Bond.

SOTHEBY'S, the famous auction house established in 1744, is located in a fine 19th century building at number 34-35 New Bond. Check to see when and what will be auctioned if you are interested in attending.

Cartier and Tiffany display magnificent jewels. Just beyond is the leather shop, Gucci.

New Bond Street has now become Old Bond Street, built by Sir Thomas Bond in 1686. Look for the **Royal Arcade** on your right. It is a kind of mini-Burlington Arcade and has nice shops including a fine book binding society. At the entrance is Charbonnel & Walker's, famous for chocolates, truffles and rose and violet creams.

You are now on Piccadilly again with the **Burlington** ⑤ **Arcade** on your left and **Fortnum and Mason's** across the street. The Arcade was built by the third Earl of Burlington in 1819 to stop the rabble throwing rubbish into his garden, goes the story. Some of the shops are owned by descendants of the original owners, although they no longer live in rooms above the shops. You can find lovely, though expensive things from one end to the other.

Note particularly the cashmeres at both of the Peal shops and the lovely hankies in the Irish Linen shop.

NOON

I AM ASSUMING, unless you never found your way out of Liberty's, that you could make this circle in a morning. It should be about noon and you are in front of **Fortnum** ⑥ **& Mason's.** If you arrive at noon, take the time to watch the Fortnum and Mason clock chime the hour. Mr. F. and Mr. M. walk out of the clock, one carrying a tray, one a candelabra, all to the sound of bells playing the Eton Boating Song

There is a nice restaurant in Fortnum and Mason's mezzanine which I like, and a much fancier one on an upper floor, which I don't. I have had poor food and miserable service upstairs, but downstairs is always pleasant and inexpensive.

Be sure to spend some time in Fortnum and Mason's.

I love to call it a grocery store. But it is unlike any other grocery store you ever saw with its tail-coated clerks and its produce, which includes such things as quail eggs. It is easy to believe they provided groceries for the Duke of Wellington's officers during the Napoleonic Wars and that they still purvey food to the royal family.

There are several upper floors with clothing and other goods, but it is the first floor grocery where you will want to spend time. They also have a corner for ordering and mailing packages of their special items to friends abroad. It is a wonderful way to provide gifts without having to carry them. The chutneys, mustards and shortbreads all make fine gifts.

AFTERNOON

Next to Fortnum and Mason's is Swaine, Adeney Brigg and Co., with leather goods, expensive umbrellas and incredible riding equipment. It is worth a look.

Hatchard's bookstore is just beyond. I happen to like this book store a great deal. It has a large stock of well-chosen books and is so much more manageable than Foyle's bookstore, which you will see tomorrow. They will mail your book selections overseas, which is a great service and eliminates a lot of heavy additions to your luggage.

Walk west on Picadilly Circus to St. James's Street. Turn left and walk on down the street, past all the private clubs with their bay and bow windows to St. James's Place.

Back to St. James's Street, turn right and walk down to number 7-9 Lobb's, England's most famous shoemaker and number 6 next door, Lock & Co., established in 1700 and still making hats. Walk into each shop, perhaps not so much to buy but to look.

On past little Pickering Place, where the last duel in England was fought, and on to number 3 **Berry Bros and Rudd,** wine merchants, founded in 1680, although their present location only dates from 1730.

Back up St. James's Street to King Street. Walk up Duke Street to Jermyn Street and turn right.

The Forte Crest St. James Hotel is on your right. Walk on to Floris, perfumers to the queen; Paxton & Whitfield with their hams and cheese, and all the fine gentlemen's shops and hairdressers.

Every shop is worth a look.

EVENING

SINCE YOU have been on your feet almost all day, try to go back for a rest in your hotel, then plan a leisurely dinner. If you don't want to give up quite yet, walk down Haymarket Street, cross **Trafalgar Square** and angle ⑦ down Northumberland Avenue to Victoria Embankment and the Thames River.

There is a restaurant ship tied up at **Charing Cross** ⑨ **Pier**, right at the end of Northumberland Avenue: The **Hispaniola** floating restaurant specializes in seafood and ⑩ game. Dinners will run about $40 per person. Or you can sit on the top deck of the Hispaniola and just have a drink and enjoy the scenery.

DAY 2

Highlights: Charing Cross Road and its great book stores, Covent Garden, and Neal's Yard.

Reservations: Lunch at Beoty's, 79 St. Martin's Lane, Telephone 020 7836-8768. Or lunch at Rules restaurant, Maiden Lane. Telephone 020 7497 1081.

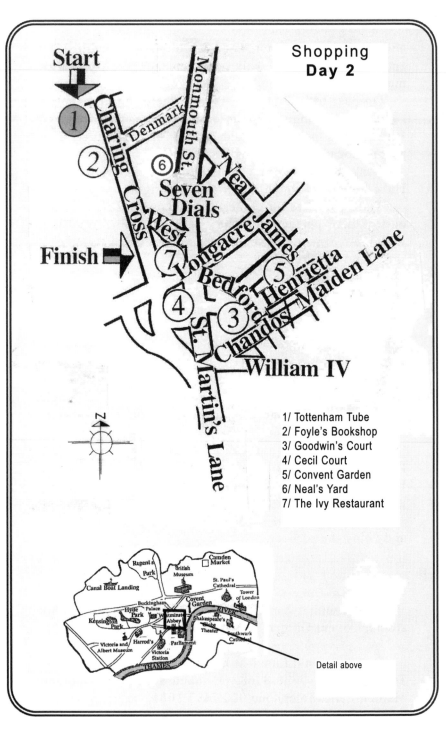

Start

Finish

Shopping
Day 2

① Charing Cross
②
Denmark
Monmouth St.
⑥ Seven Dials
Neal
West
Longacre
James
⑦ Bedford
Henrietta
Maiden Lane
⑤
④ Chandos
③
St. Martin's Lane
William IV

N

1/ Tottenham Tube
2/ Foyle's Bookshop
3/ Goodwin's Court
4/ Cecil Court
5/ Convent Garden
6/ Neal's Yard
7/ The Ivy Restaurant

Regent's Park
Camden Market
British Museum
St. Paul's Cathedral
Canal Boat Landing
Tower of London
Buckingham Palace
Covent Garden
Hyde Park
Westminster Abbey
RIVER
Kensington Park
Shakespeare's Globe Theater
Southwark Cathedral
Victoria and Albert Museum
Harrod's
Parliament
Victoria Station
THAMES

Detail above

Dinner at The Ivy, West Street. Telephone 020 7836-4715.

MORNING

START at the **Tottenham Court Road** tube stop this morning, which is at the north end of Charing Cross Road. Today you will visit book stores, tiny, winding old streets and alleys and Covent Garden.

Charing Cross is the street for scholars and musicians with its dozens of book and records stores. I will note some of the ones I particularly like.

Walk south on Charing Cross to **Foyles** bookstore on the corner of Charing Cross and little Manette Street. Remember Dicken's Dr. Manette in a *Tale of Two Cities?* Foyles is rumored to have more than 4 million books, which I have no reason to disbelieve. I love wandering around this store and hate waiting to pay for the books I want. They had the most incredibly antiquated business system in the world. But it has been recently updated with new elevators and stairs and a really good café next to Ray's Jazz Shop on the first floor.

Beyond Foyle's at number 100 is Blackwell's, an academic book chain, but it also features current bestsellers at good prices.

Several blocks on you will come to Shipley Design & Architecture (formerly called Zwemmer) with its fine design books. Next door at 70 Charing Cross is Shipley with its traditional bestsellers and run by people who really know their business.

Murder One is at number 71-73 Charing Cross...two stories filled with crime, mystery and horror novels.

At 48A Charing Cross is Francis Edwards Quinto's bookshop which is paired with its antiquarian book shop next door. You could look forever.

At this point you will have arrived at the Leicester Square Tube station. Continue to **Goodwin's Court** on your left. You will have to look very carefully for the entry to this court. This is one of the special places in

London with its row of late 18th century Regency buildings with their bow windows. Potted bay trees line the
walk way.

④   Walk back to St. Martin's Lane, turn left for a half
block, and on your right is **Cecil Court**, 1670. Just before
you get there you will see the Victorian Salisbury Pub.
Depending on your time, you may want to stop. This high
camp pub is decorated with glass and mirrors and lots of
gilt.

Cecil Court is filled with print and book shops and
other nice little places. Check out Nigel Williams Rare
Books, combined with the children's book collector, (formerly at 22 Cecil Court) at 25 Cecil Court. Look for its
rare first editions including first of *The Lord of the Rings.*

Check out Watkins at Number 21 for mystery and
occult books and Bell, and P.J. Hilton at Number 12 for its
used books.

NOON

Time to eat. You can walk down St. Martin's Lane to
Number 79 and the Greek restaurant, **Beoty's.** Very
nice. Or continue down St. Martin's to William IV Street,
which intersects with Chandos Place. Walk straight ahead
until Chandos turns into Maiden Lane and continue to the
old English restaurant, **Rules.** Lovely food.

If you want a pub lunch, try the **Maple Leaf Pub** next
to Rules. It is very popular and crowded for a very good
reason. It is excellent, the service pleasant and the atmosphere friendly and welcoming.

AFTERNOON

This afternoon: the 400-year-old **Covent Garden.**
⑤   Originally, this was the convent garden of
Westminster Abbey. In 1662, Charles II granted charters
to two theater companies which still operate here.

Theatre Royal Drury Lane opened in 1663 and the
Covent Garden theatre, now the **Royal Opera House,**

opened in 1732. In 1672, the Earl of Bedford received a charter to open a market for fruits, vegetables and flowers which operated until it moved to Nine Elms in 1974.

The once-abandoned area has been converted into a flourishing array of shops, galleries, restaurants and theaters.

Walk up to the market from wherever you have had lunch. Although your prime interest today is in the shops, take time to walk in and around **St. Paul's Church** with its famous portico where the fictional Professor Higgins met his Fair Lady, Eliza Doolittle.

I am not even going to attempt to suggest what you should see during your perambulations around the two-level market. It is filled with book and clothing stores, restaurants and pubs and specialty shops such as Pollock's Toy Theater. This is an all-afternoon excursion.

After you finish shopping at The Market, walk north on James Street and Neal Street to find a variety of different craft shops and to **Neal's Yard,** a tiny flower-filled courtyard with health foodshops, crafts and a restaurant. ⑥

EVENING

IF YOU WANT DINNER in this area, I can think of no finer place than **The Ivy** on West Street. Walk back to Seven ⑦ Dials, the star-shaped intersection where seven streets meet. (There was once a column here containing seven sundials.) Walk down to St. Martin's Theater, turn right on West Street. The Ivy is located just opposite the Ambassador Theater where Agatha Christie's *The Mousetrap* has been playing since 1953.

Or, just let your late afternoon tea take the place of dinner, and go to the theatre this evening. Check your newspapers for the current schedules and playing times. For something different, check what is playing at the **Donmar Warehouse Theatre**, which is in this area. You may see an interesting contemporary play in London's version of an Off-Off Broadway theatre.

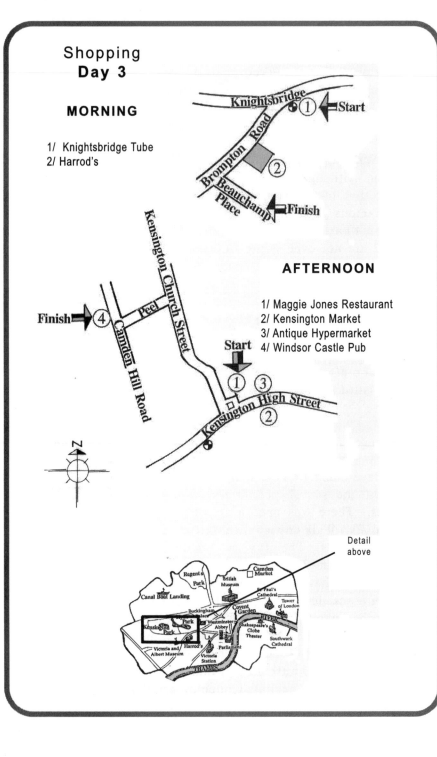

Shopping
Day 3

MORNING

1/ Knightsbridge Tube
2/ Harrod's

AFTERNOON

1/ Maggie Jones Restaurant
2/ Kensington Market
3/ Antique Hypermarket
4/ Windsor Castle Pub

Detail above

DAY 3

Highlights: Knightsbridge and Harrod's Department Store, Beauchamp Place, Kensington High Street and Church Street.

Reservations: Lunch at Maggie Jones, 6 Old Court Place. Telephone 020 7376 0510. Dinner at The English Garden, 10 Lincoln St., Sloane Square Tube. Telephone 020 7584 7272.

MORNING

THE **KNIGHTSBRIDGE TUBE STOP** is the starting point for ① today's adventure. Today you are going to shop the **Knightsbridge area**, where the greatest department store in Europe is located, and then go to the Kensington area.

Just opposite the tube stop at the intersection of Knightsbridge and Brompton road is the elegant department store, Harvey Nichols; across the street is the Scotch House.

The **Scotch House** has one of my favorite rooms in London. It is a beautiful dark-panelled circular room with shelves from top to bottom.Each shelf has a bolt of woolen material woven with one of the famous Scottish clan plaids. it is incredible to see them all in one place. I had no idea there were so many clans.

Walk down **Brompton Road**, not Knightsbridge. Somehow, this is one place where I always get turned around; watch the signs. Walk about three blocks, past Fiorucci's, Benetton (not so exotic now that they are on every block in the United States) and Charles Jourdan and the pedestrian Scholl's footcare place. I do not know what I would do without their comforting lambswool and other products, which so lovingly care for my most precious possessions as I walk around London.

Keep going, past a number of small shops and then you are at **Harrods,** the Department Store, so popular that ②

it is often very crowded. The food halls are the number
one attraction, with artistic displays of fruits, vegetables
and fish that are marvels of ingenuity. The hanging car-
casses of beasts and fowls, the hundreds of tempting
cheeses, the confectioneries, and the dozens of pates are
mind boggling. Notice the beautiful tiles set in the walls
and ceilings. You can investigate the upper floors for
clothing, books and all kinds of other wonderful things.
Harrod's has one of the best tourist information desks in
town.

And if you want to get your hair done, this is the
place. Fine hairdressers and tea while you wait.

In 1989 Harrod's adopted a new dress policy banning
short shorts, revealing tops and cut-off jeans. Tailored
shorts or Bermuda shorts are acceptable. Guards at the 11
entrances to the store are under orders to inspect shoppers
and turn away those unsuitably dressed.

H OW DO YOU FOLLOW an act like Harrod's? Walk south
on Brompton Road to little **Beauchamp Place** with
its Regency shops and iron balconies. It is just the right
antidote for all that elegance and puffery. I love this little
street with its charming shops.

The **Map House** is one of my favorite browsing store
of its kind. Climb up to the second floor for additional
exploring. At the end of Beauchamp Place, you will come
to Walton Street, which is filled with fashionable shops,
pubs and residences.

You can walk in either direction on Walton Street to
explore its elegant shops and charming buildings.

NOON

① G RAB A CAB to Kensington high Street and Number 6
Old Court Place for lunch at **Maggie Jones.** No frills,
wooden tables and sawdust on the floor, but they have
very good food. Lunch will be moderate. Or, if you can't
break away from Beauchamp Place, there are a number of

eating places along the street.

AFTERNOON

KENSINGTON HIGH STREET has been a busy highway since Roman times, and is still popular. The Kensington High Street tube stop is now part of a fine shopping arcade with Marks & Spencer at the entrance.

Just opposite Old Court Place, where you may have just had lunch at Maggie Jones, is the **Kensington** ②
Market with 40 boutiques and 150 stalls for antiques and current fashions. The **Antique Hypermarket** is opposite ③
it. They can both take hours of your time.

Rather than continue down Kensington High Street west of the tube stop, I suggest you return to Kensington Church Street, which winds and climbs the hill past antique shops, book stores and art shops of all kinds.

Walk up Church Street until you get tired or until you get to Peel Street.

Turn left and walk to the Campden Hill Road. On the corner is the **Windsor Castle Pub**, built in 1835. This is ④
the highest point of Campden Hill and at one time it was claimed you could see Windsor Castle from its windows.

Try the **Campden Bar** with its early 19th century window. When you are ready to leave, hail a cab.

EVENING

GO BACK TO YOUR HOTEL and rest a bit before taking off for your dinner at **The English Garden**, 10 Lincoln St., Chelsea. It has a garden room with a domed glass roof.

EXTRA DAY

Highlights: Portobello Market, Camden Passage Market, Petticoat Lane and Bermondsey Market

THIS IS THAT FOURTH DAY I promised you for London's great markets on Fridays, Saturdays and Sundays. On

Friday, the **junk market** south of the Thames at Bermondsey starts early, at 4 a.m. and goes on till noon. They say that if you look carefully, you may find bargains but you have to go early.

My favorite is **Portobello**, Notting Hill tube stop, on Saturday mornings. I know it is corny and crowded and there are no bargains, but I love it and the challenge of trying to find a bargain.

There are shops/stalls which sell coffee, sweets and other foods. Oranges and strawberries vie with derbies, leather jackets, silver and toast racks. Master butchers display whole pigs and pork bellies; the hot bread shop sells scone rings.

A good combination of markets is Portobello on Saturday morning and **Camden Passage** market in the afternoon, even though they are miles apart. I have to admit when I did this, I took a cab, which was a bit expensive, but so convenient.

Y OU CAN TAKE the **Circle Line** tube from Notting Hill tube stop to Moorgate and transfer to the **Northern line** to Angel. It does take extra time but is not as expensive as my beloved cab.

Camden operates all week, but like many markets, Saturday is the big day. They have regular indoor shops, but on Saturday, there are dozens of outdoor stalls. Here is one of the places to look for antiques and silver. Probably no great bargains, but fun, and there are a number of good restaurants here.

O n Sunday, if you love flea markets and the junk shops, try **Petticoat Lane** on Middlesex Street. Tube stops are either Aldgate or Aldgate East. (Sunday from early hours to 2 p.m; serious shoppers start at 4 a.m.)

I still remember one rainy Sunday morning when I tried to eat jellied eel which I bought at Tubby Isaac's stand. It was simply disgusting; one of the few foods I could just not handle.

S hopping in London can be as elegant or ordinary as you desire. Your choices are infinite. I have only scratched the surface.

Two final suggestions: The shops attached to museums, many of the churches and other points of interest, are almost all first rate and worth a visit.

And the last suggestion is to purchase the very inexpensive guides on famous places published by Pitkin Pictorials Ltd. and available at the places they describe and from booksellers in London. They are beautifully printed with intelligent text and exquisite color photographs and may prove the finest memory gifts you can bring home.

Good hunting.

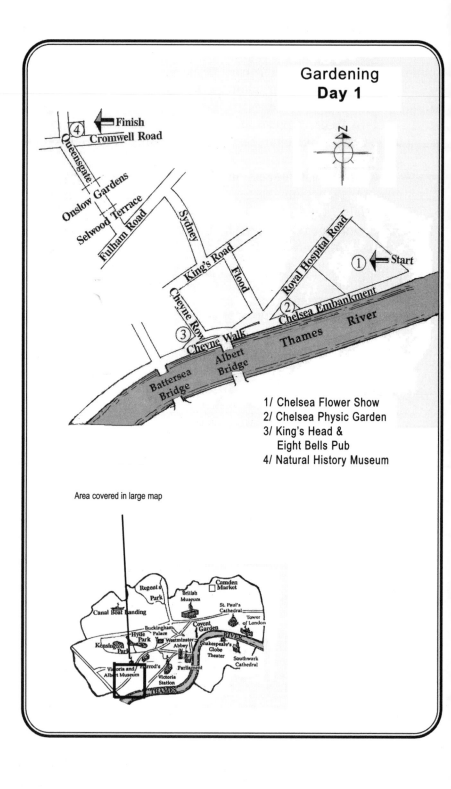

Gardening
Day 1

Finish
Cromwell Road

Queensgate

Onslow Gardens

Selwood Terrace

Fulham Road

Sydney

King's Road

Flood

Cheyne Row

Royal Hospital Road

Start

Chelsea Embankment

Cheyne Walk

Thames River

Battersea Bridge

Albert Bridge

1/ Chelsea Flower Show
2/ Chelsea Physic Garden
3/ King's Head &
   Eight Bells Pub
4/ Natural History Museum

Area covered in large map

Regent's Park

Camden Market

British Museum

St. Paul's Cathedral

Canal Boat Landing

Tower of London

Buckingham Palace

Covent Garden

Hyde Park

Westminster Abbey

Kensington Park

Shakespeare's Globe Theater

Southwark Cathedral

Victoria and Albert Museum

Harrod's

Parliament

Victoria Station

THAMES

GARDENER'S
LONDON

In London's green crown,
discover some special jewels

IF AN ENGLISHMAN'S HOME is his castle, his garden is his pride. No matter where you go in England, you will find gardens.

They may be rose bushes or rhododendrons massed together on postage-sized lots adjacent to tiny cottages or magnificent gardens designed by the famous landscape architect, Lancelot Brown, better known as Capability Brown. Brown received his nickname because of his habit of saying that any commission had great capabilities.

It is no wonder that gardeners throughout the world know of England's passion for plants and flowers and come to visit the dozens of great gardens throughout the country. But you do not have to leave London and its environs to see magnificent plantings. Three days are not long enough to do more than see some of the highlights, but it should give you a sufficient taste to lure you back for more.

One of these three days will be spent in the outskirts of London. It is easy to get to these gardens by public transportation, but you may want to rent a car for the day for more flexibility.

To see the gardens at their height of bloom and to take

advantage of visiting the great Chelsea Flower Show, visit London in the spring, preferably in May. If this is not possible, do not fret.

London blooms from May to October.

If you are interested in visiting private gardens, write for a booklet describing them and the process for visiting: National Gardens Scheme, 57 Lower Belgrave St., London SWI.

DAY 1

Highlights: Chelsea Flower Show, Chelsea Physic Garden, The Natural History Museum and Holland Park.

Write in Advance: Membership in the Royal Horticulture Society. Write Royal Horticulture Society, 80 Vincent Square, London SWIP 2PE.

Reservations. Lunch: In the last edition of this book I recommended La Tante Claire at 68 Royal Hospital Road at the corner of Swan Walk. This is now the site of Gordon Ramsay's great restaurant: **Gordon Ramsay** at 68 Royal Hospital Road. Telephone 020-7352 4441. This is expensive and usually crowded. If you want a great meal and are willing to pay a premium, this is very special. They do have a prix-fixe lunch for about $60. You see, I said it was expensive, but extraordinary.

Open air theater performance at Holland Park from June through August. Telephone 020 633-1707.

MORNING

① THIS DAY IS PREDICATED on timing your trip to coincide with the **Chelsea Flower Show**, which is held four days in May. Each year you must check to find out the exact days, usually after May 20. Have your travel agent check the dates.

The first day of the four days of the flower show is reserved for members of the Royal Horticulture Society.

You might want to consider joining, about $20 per person. Your membership provides a free ticket for member's day at the flower show and a subscription to their monthly publication, *The Gardener.*

When you realize about 70,000 people attend each of the public days, a membership might be a very good idea.

The Chelsea Flower Show, which began in 1913, is held on the grounds of **Chelsea's Royal Hospital,** where more than 400 pensioners still live. You will recognize them by their ornate red or blue 18th-century uniforms. During the show, these spacious grounds are filled with acres of floral displays from all over the world. The Royal Horticultural Society staff is present to answer questions.

To get there, either tube to the **Sloane Street** station and take a rather long walk down Lower Sloane Street, where you will turn right on Royal Hospital Road. Or, take a cab.

The grounds open at 8:00 a.m.; go early. You will probably spend the entire morning or longer at the show. If you choose to spend the entire day, you can skip the rest of these suggestions and plan to cab to Holland Park for dinner,

I will not attempt to walk you through the show, since each year it is different. There will be many unofficial guides to direct you. This is a once in a lifetime experience for the avid gardener. The show usually is open from 8 a.m. to 8 p.m., except for the final day when it closes at 5 p.m. after the sale of exhibits to the public.

NOON

IF YOU CHOOSE to leave at noon, walk down the **Royal Hospital Road.** It is probably time to eat. I suggest either a rather expensive restaurant, **Gordon Ramsay** at 68 Royal Hospital Road, or at a nearby pub.

Or you can continue down the road, which becomes the Chelsea Embankment, till you arrive at Cheyne Row where you will find the pub called **King's Head & Eight** ③

Bells on the corner. This is an appropriate place today because you can drink and snack in a garden overlooking the Thames, or eat in an upstairs restaurant. The food is excellent and not expensive.

AFTERNOON

②   THE **CHELSEA PHYSIC GARDEN**, on the Royal Hospital Road, was founded in 1673 for the study of horticulture. (Open during the Chelsea Flower Show from 11 a.m. to 2 p.m.; other times of the year, open Wednesday and Sunday from 2 to 5 p.m. At other times you must apply for access by writing to the Clerk to the Trustees, 10 Fleet St, London, EC 4.)

This is a special garden. I saw it by accident one day when the gardeners had left the door open, and I just walked in. Its research over the last several hundred years has supplied Georgia's cotton seeds via plants from the South seas; India's tea and quinine from China and South America; and Malaysia's rubber plants from South America. You can walk back a few blocks from the pub to see this garden.

Walk north through Chelsea on Flood Street, cross King's Road. Turn left about two blocks and turn left on Sydney Street. Walk through South Kensington to see the informal gardens.

When Sydney Street reaches Fulham Road, turn left and walk to Selwood Terrace/Neville Terrace, turn right. This street becomes Queen's Gate Road. Queen's Gate ends at Cromwell Road where you will find the **Natural History Museum.**

④   Visit the **Botanical Department** on the second floor with its dioramas showing different kinds of habitats in the British Isles and other places, including an African rain forest and the Arizona desert.

EVENING

THIS EVENING I suggest dinner and/or the open air theatre performance in **Holland Park**. Go back to your hotel to rest and then cab to Holland Park in time for dinner and the open air theatre production.

This flower garden with its exotic peacocks and geese is open from dawn to dusk. Give yourself time to wander through the gardens. Be sure to see the Kyoto Garden, a Japanese-styled area. There is an Orangery with exhibitions and poetry readings, often concerts on the lawn.

Near the gardens are the arcades which now contain an art gallery and restaurant, plus a simpler café.

The **open air theater** is held in a courtyard in front of a ruined house which was bombed in 1941 and never restored. The grounds, with its more than 3,000 species of trees and plants, has been kept up.

DAY 2

Highlights: Kew Gardens, and Syon House.

Reservations: Dinner at one of two lovely garden restaurants: The Greenhouse, 27a Hays Mews. Telephone 020 7499 5368; or The Roof Garden, 99 Kensington High Street, entrance on Derry Street. Located over British Home Stores. Laid out in the 1930s in three sections: Spanish, Tudor and a water garden, whose fountain is fed by an artesian well. Open only for dinner on Thursdays and Saturdays. Reservations essential (0171) 937 7994. Extraordinary gardens.

MORNING

TODAY IS YOUR DAY outside of London. You are going to the Royal Botanic Gardens, known as Kew Gardens and Syon House and Gardens.

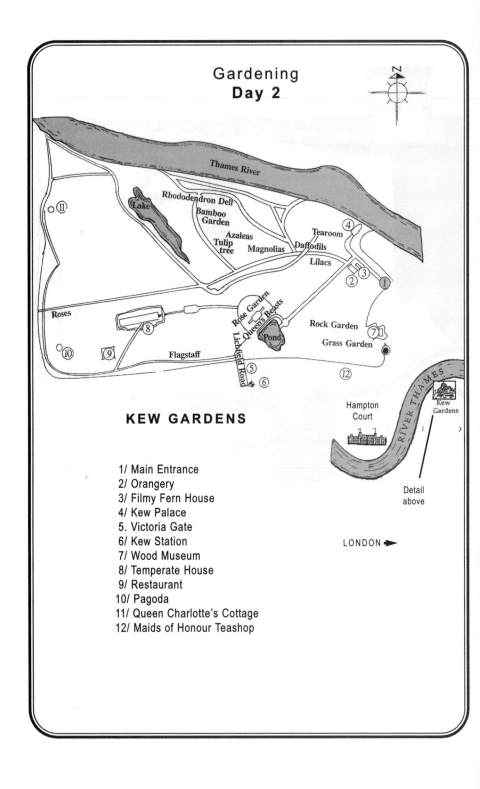

Gardening
Day 2

N

Thames River

Lake

Rhododendron Dell

Bamboo Garden

Azaleas
Tulip tree

Magnolias

Daffodils

Tearoom

④

⑪

Lilacs

② ③

①

Roses

Rose Garden

Queen's Beasts

Pond

Rock Garden

⑦

Grass Garden

⑧

Flagstaff

⑩

⑨

Lichfield Road

⑤

⑥

⑫

KEW GARDENS

Hampton Court

Kew Gardens

RIVER THAMES

Detail above

LONDON ➤

1/ Main Entrance
2/ Orangery
3/ Filmy Fern House
4/ Kew Palace
5. Victoria Gate
6/ Kew Station
7/ Wood Museum
8/ Temperate House
9/ Restaurant
10/ Pagoda
11/ Queen Charlotte's Cottage
12/ Maids of Honour Teashop

You can reach **Kew Gardens** by the Tube (underground); the District Line going to Richmond will also take you there. The trip lasts about half an hour, so plan to leave in time to reach the gardens when they open at 9:30 a.m. Closing times vary, earlier in the winter 4:30 and 6:30 during the summer months. The gardens are a five minute walk from the Kew Garden tube stop.

If the weather is beautiful and you want to take the time, the river trip to the gardens is the most beautiful way to go. Boats leave from Westminster pier and take about an hour and one half.

I think spring is the best time to visit these 288 acres. There are refreshments in the summer at the Pavilion and at a kiosk near the main gate.

YOUR SPECIFIC WALK will depend on your point of arrival; there are a number of gates through which you can enter the gardens. If you take the tube and walk straight up Lichfield Road, you will arrive at the **Victoria Gate.** ⑤

If you take the boat you will probably enter at the **main gate.** ①

The map will give you an idea of where the special plantings and houses are located, but may not give you an idea of the size of the place. Even telling you that it is 288 acres may not do it. I assure you it is huge.

Let me make a few suggestions and then you pick out the places which appeal to you the most. Just remember it is a long walk from the main gate to Queen Charlotte's cottage.

Personally, I like the outdoor gardens better than the museums and glass houses. I love the pond with its Chinese guardian lions and the Queen's Beasts, the Rose Garden and the lake with its wonderful birds.

Kew Palace with its Dutch rooms is not very interesting to me, but I like the **Filmy Fern House** and all the rock and grass gardens. The Temperate House is the usual indoor botanical garden. ④ ③

Very frankly, unless you are in great walking shape I would forego the far reaches of the garden with **Queen Charlotte's Cottage** at one end and the Pagoda at the other, neither of which can you enter.

⑪

② Head for the **Orangery** first to get the newest map. The book's map should give you a good idea of where things are, but cannot tell you what will be in bloom or what is open on the day of your visit.

NOON

IT WILL TAKE the whole morning for just a cursory walk through these magnificent gardens. When you get hungry, either eat on the grounds or walk down Kew Road to the **Maids of Honour Teashop**. It usually has a single choice of soup and main dish for lunch, but also has a lovely bakery where I like to buy their maids of honour, little round flaky almond pastries.

⑫

Or, cross Kew Bridge and turn right to reach Shand on Green and one of its historic pubs. Either the **City Barge** or the **Bull's Eye Pub** will help alleviate your hunger.

YOU CAN SPEND your entire day in the gardens or you can visit Syon house and gardens. If you have a car, you can cross the Kew Bridge and go on to **Syon Park.** If you are on foot, cross the Kew Bridge to Kew Bridge Road where you can take bus 237 or 267 to Brent Lea and Syon Park and House. Check the bus route, they do change there just as in every place in the world.

The **Syon House** grounds are open daily from 11 a.m. to 5 or sunset. The rose gardens are open from May to August and have a separate entrance south of the house. The grounds here are the oldest horticultural gardens in England, older than Kew. The were begun in the 16th century with mulberry trees imported from the continent. Our old friend, Capability Brown, started here before moving over to Kew. The gardens are magnificent. Just wander around.

Be sure to visit the **garden center**, which is the super-market of gardens. There is a conservatory with birds and an aquarium. The Butterfly House (open from 10 a.m. to 5 p.m.) across from the supermarket, is very hot, humid and sort of tacky, but is still fun. It was the first time I was ever surrounded by these pretty fluttering creatures. I do love the sign at the exit: Check your clothes for resting butterflies.

Even though your main interest is gardens, do visit **Syon House**, at least the first five rooms, which were designed by Robert Adams for the Duke of Northumberland. The house is open Wednesday, Thursday and Sunday from 11 a.m. to 5 p.m.

The Classical entry hall leads you into a magnificent anteroom, worthy of a Caesar, with its gild-ings, carvings and huge columns. You then walk into the dining room, which reverts to almost total white except for some gilding around the statues in the niches. Then you arrive at the magnificent red drawing room and the gallery from which you can view Kew Gardens.

You can leave at this point; the rest is a let down after Adam's splendid rooms.

To return, retrace your steps to the underground sta-tion or drive back. The same buses, 237 or 267, will take you back to the tube stop or boat landing. Again, check the bus numbers...just ask the driver.

EVENING

YOU WILL HAVE DONE a great deal of walking today and probably will be very tired. For a lovely relaxing dinner tonight, go to one of the **garden restaurants** pre-viously suggested.

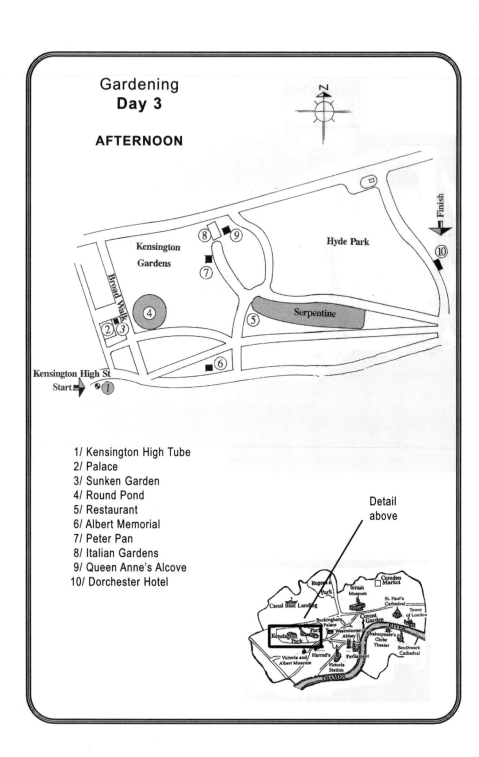

Gardening
Day 3

AFTERNOON

Kensington Gardens

Hyde Park

Broad Walk

Serpentine

Round Pond ④

Kensington High St
Start

Finish

1/ Kensington High Tube
2/ Palace
3/ Sunken Garden
4/ Round Pond
5/ Restaurant
6/ Albert Memorial
7/ Peter Pan
8/ Italian Gardens
9/ Queen Anne's Alcove
10/ Dorchester Hotel

Detail
above

DAY 3

Highlights: Regent's Park and Kensington Gardens.

Reservation: Dinner at the Bombay Brasserie, Courtfield Close. Telephone 020 7835 1669.

MORNING

START THE DAY by going to **Regent's Park**. Plan to arrive about 10 a.m. The closest tube stops are either Baker Street or Regent's Park. Walk down Marylebone Road to York Street and the main entrance to the park and **Queen Mary's Gardens.**

The rose gardens are in their glory from May to July, and often into the fall. The beauty of the roses and the incredible scent is overwhelming. I could spend hours here. When you can wrench yourself away, you will find a Japanese garden on an island in a little lake.

The other flower beds in the park are much more formal, but have stunning displays which change, depending on the time of year.

An open air theatre, where Shakespeare is performed in the summer, is located in this magical setting. The **Rose Garden Restaurant** will provide mid-morning sustenance. Just wander around to your heart's content in this special place.

NOON

TAKE A TUBE to **HIGH STREET KENSINGTON**, an easy ride ① from Baker Street on the Circle Line, or take a cab to Kensington High Street. For lunch, go to **Maggie Jones** on 6 Old Court Place.

It is old and funky but has excellent food and a lively crowd at noon.

AFTERNOON

W ALK UP Kensington High Street to Kensington Gardens. Turn left on the Broad Walk and continue to **Kensington Palace.**

② ④ ③

The **Round Pond** will be on your right and the **Palace**, with its Orangery and **sunken gardens**, on your left.

Walk across the park, toward **The Serpentine**, a lake which winds between Kensington Gardens and Hyde Park.

⑦ ⑧

When you arrive at the water, turn left and walk along the Serpentine to the **Peter Pan** statue, the **Italian Gardens** and **Queen Anne's Alcove.**

⑨

You can spend the afternoon exploring the 288 acres of this garden or you can wander into adjacent **Hyde Park** and explore an equally large green space.

There is a **restaurant** next to the bridge crossing the Serpentine in case you want something to eat or drink, or you can walk across Hyde Park to Park Lane and the **Dorchester Hotel** for an elegant cream tea.

EVENING

L ATER IN THE EVENING, cab to the **Bombay Brasserie** on Courtfield Close, SW7, to spend the evening in an elegant reconstruction of the British Raj with its white wicker furniture and gorgeous plantings. It is expensive but worth it....over $100 for two if you don't drink anything expensive.

Y OUR THREE DAYS of gardening in London have come to an end, but you have barely touched the surface. Great things are still in store for you.

London is blessed with many other wonderful parks and green places. **Green Park** and **St. James's Park**, with its exotic flowers and birds, are in the middle of the city.

Just a few minutes from the center of the city are **Greenwich Park** in the southeast and Richmond Park in the southwest. **Battersea Park**, just south of the Thames, features a boating lake, Henry Moore sculptures and a sub-tropical garden.

And of course there are the newly renovated **Jubilee Gardens,** on the south side of the Thames adjacent to **The London Eye** — the 450-foot high "Ferris Wheel." I know the Londoners would hate having me call it that, but it is descriptive and one of the city's new wonders.

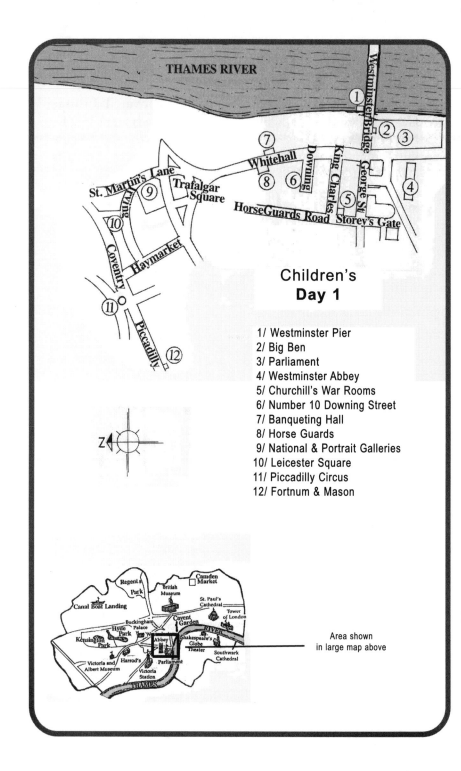

THAMES RIVER

Children's
Day 1

1/ Westminster Pier
2/ Big Ben
3/ Parliament
4/ Westminster Abbey
5/ Churchill's War Rooms
6/ Number 10 Downing Street
7/ Banqueting Hall
8/ Horse Guards
9/ National & Portrait Galleries
10/ Leicester Square
11/ Piccadilly Circus
12/ Fortnum & Mason

Area shown
in large map above

CHILDREN'S LONDON

What's more appealing
than this special city?

L ONDON is the perfect city for children. Where else can you find castles, canals, penny arcades, the Tower of London, sailing ships, pigeons and pandas and a "ferris wheel," called The London Eye, which towers 450 feet high?

A little careful planning can help you and your children have a wonderful time together. I can think of no other city which is such a magic place for children to explore.

I arbitrarily choose to define my tour for children between the ages of six and thirteen. That's because most people will not plan to sightsee with very little children; teenagers pose a whole different set of challenges.

There is one great advantage to traveling with children: Adults get a chance to do things they might be self-conscious about doing without a kid in tow. I suspect most of us are just children in big people's clothing. My daughter, Ruth, says the only difference between grown ups and children is that children are shorter and have no money. Traveling with them will give you an additional opportunity to see the wonders of London through the unclouded eyes of your young ones.

Just a few pieces of information before you start your first day's tour. For the latest information about daily events for children you can call Kidsline 0845/458-3536 on weekdays from 9 a.m. to 4 p.m.

I suggest that people traveling with children consider renting an apartment. It is nice to have extra room, and particularly, a kitchen. Your travel agent can help locate apartments as well as hotel rooms.

In case the adults want to go off on their own, your hotel will often be able to provide or locate a reputable "child minder," which is British for baby sitter.

Most of the restaurants mentioned in this chapter will not need reservations, but if you choose others, do book tables. Some of the suggested eating places provide take away food for picnic eating.

You will save the 17 1/2 per cent VAT (Value added tax) if you consume food off the premises, a nice saving. And fish and chips make a pleasant outdoor meal.

Avoid the mobile vans on side streets; they are not always well supervised. The coffee stalls for tea, sandwiches and coffee are fine. The ice cream vans which are almost always near park entrances and other such places are fine but expensive. Try to buy your ice creams and sweets in the confectionery or tobacco shops.

Enough of the housekeeping details. Let's see London.

This first day you will start at the castle called the Tower of London, visit an underground bunker and explore London's version of penny arcades.

DAY 1

Highlights: Tower of London, Thames River, Houses of Parliament, Big Ben, Westminster Abbey, Cabinet War Rooms, Trafalgar Square, Leicester Square and Piccadilly Circus.

Reservations: No reservations necessary if you go to the restaurants I recommend in this chapter.

MORNING

Take the tube to Tower Hill or cab to the **Tower of London** (open 9 a.m. to 5 p.m., Tuesday to Saturday; 10 a.m. to 5 p.m. Sunday and Monday) in time to arrive when it opens. This many-turreted castle with its Beefeaters in their fancy uniforms, the buildings filled with armor and weapons and the ravens hopping around the grounds, all overlooking the majestic Thames River, is a child's fairytale come true.

The **Beefeaters**, the guards for the tower, lead free one-hour tours. Take the tour and enjoy both the magnificent sights and the history your guides provide en route. Incidentally, one extra sight the guides might not mention is the empty raven cages located just beyond the Bloody Tower.

The ravens spend their nights in the cages. As you probably know, the story goes that if the ravens ever leave the tower, England will fall. They never have and probably never will; their wings are clipped.

NOON

Take the walk in front of the tower to see the display of cannons and the **outdoor cafe** along the river. This is a lovely place to eat with a spectacular view.

AFTERNOON

Walk back to Tower pier and take one of the **river boats** to **Westminster Pier**, about a 20-minute ride. ① Climb the steps from the pier and walk out on Westminster Bridge to see the famous view of the **Houses of** ② **Parliament, Big Ben, Westminster Abbey** and the river ③ Thames.

Walk down Bridge Street to the North Door of the ④ **Abbey.** Admission is charged (about $10 for adults; $5 for children and seniors..there is also a family price.

Admire the lofty ceiling, great stained glass windows and dozens of chapels and statues. Wander through without spending too much time reading labels or worrying about what is what. Just enjoy the extraordinary beauty of the place.

Check to see if they still have a Brass Rubbing Center. If not, we will visit a rubbing center near Trafalgar Square.

⑤ WALK TO Storey's Gate, which becomes Horse Guards Road, to King Charles Street. Turn right and you will find the entrance to the **Cabinet War Rooms**, from which Prime Minister Winston Churchill directed Britain's activities in World War II. They are located ten feet underground in the basement of the government offices. Although a few rooms had been open to visitors on a restricted basis, at least 17 rooms were opened to the public in 1985. Since then additional rooms have opened including Churchill's private kitchen and dining room and Mrs. Churchill's bedroom.

The bunker is open daily 10 a.m. to 6 p.m., last admission 5:15 p.m., with an admission charge of about $10 for adults, $8 for seniors and students, free for children 16 and under. You will receive a map of the complex; you will also have a recorded sound guide.

Of particular interest are the map room, the nerve center of the operation; the Trans-Atlantic telephone room and the Prime Minister's bedroom. There are exhibitions and memorabilia in a number of the rooms. In Room 64 note the sign-in book with its very first entry: 29 May 1942 Dwight D. Eisenhower, Major-General, USA.

⑥
⑦ WALK UP King Charles Street to Parliament Street which becomes Whitehall. Turn left and walk past **Number 10 Downing Street**, the **Banqueting Hall** on your right, the **Horse Guards** on your left. Enjoy walking
⑧ into the Horse Guards courtyard with its clocktower. Two mounted troopers are on guard at all times.

Walk straight on to **Trafalgar Square** with its fountains, Nelson's Column, the tourists and hundreds of pigeons. The pigeons are tame, almost too tame if you are not crazy about birds. You can get your picture taken with a pigeon on your arm or your head, if you can stand it. Your kids will love it.

MID-AFTERNOON SNACK

IT IS probably time to eat again. Walk up Haymarket Street to **Piccadilly Circus**, where you will find the ⑪ famous statue of Eros, the Greek god of love. and hundreds of young people sitting nearby.

Turn left on Piccadilly and walk to **Fortnum and Mason**, open since 1707, but recently treated to a multi-⑫ million dollar renovation. Make your way to their fountain restaurant. Here you'll find good and inexpensive sandwiches, pastries and the best sodas in London. The children will love seeing the grocery clerks in morning coats with baskets over their arms selecting groceries for distinguished looking women. Not quite like home.

Or you could walk into **St Martin-in-the-Fields** church, on the northeast corner of Trafalger Square. Walk down the inside steps to the crypt which is paved with gravestones, walls from the 1500's, a nice restaurant, **Café in the Crypt**, (what else would it be called) and my promised **Brass Rubbing Center**. They have more than 80 exact copies of bronze images, and all the rubbing materials, plus instructions. It costs between $5 and $25, depending on the size. There is also a nice gift shop where you can buy rubbings if you are not inclined to create your own. This is a really remarkable place.

NO MATTER which place you choose, walk back to Trafalgar and walk up St. Martin's Lane on the right of Trafalgar Square to **Leicester Square.** There are statues of a number of people on the square including a handsome one of Shakespeare.

Here you will also find the London version of Penny Arcades. Quite different from our American versions. Some are rather plain but others are quite palatial with chandeliers and carpeting. People under the age of 18 must be accompanied by an adult to enter these places.

SUPPER

Two nearby places will make you feel at home, if you want to feel "at home". **Planet Hollywood** is located in the Trocadero at 13 Coventry Street. You can eat Tex-Mex food or Cajun and burgers or even low-fat meat dishes from the rotisserie. Open daily...all day.

The **Rainforest Café** at 20 Shaftesbury Avenue is great for children. Standard family fare, but with a simulated rain forest environment. It is also open daily...all day. Try one of their "smoothies".... A really good drink.

After the penny arcades and supper, you might just want to go back to your hotel and sack out. If you have any energy left, there are always concerts and movies.

DAY 2

Highlights: Kensington Gardens and Palace, Serpentine Lake, Queen's Ice Skating Club, and the London Toy and Model Museum.

Reservations: No reservations necessary if you eat at the restaurants as recommended in this chapter. For information on evening cruises on the Thames River, telephone 020/7930 or 4097.

LET'S MOVE OVER to the other side of London for a day **outdoors.** Needless to say, these days are interchangeable depending on the weather. There is something for every child and every adult today. You can swim in the Serpentine, skate in an indoor ice rink, visit the queen's doll house, play with toys and eat fish and chips.

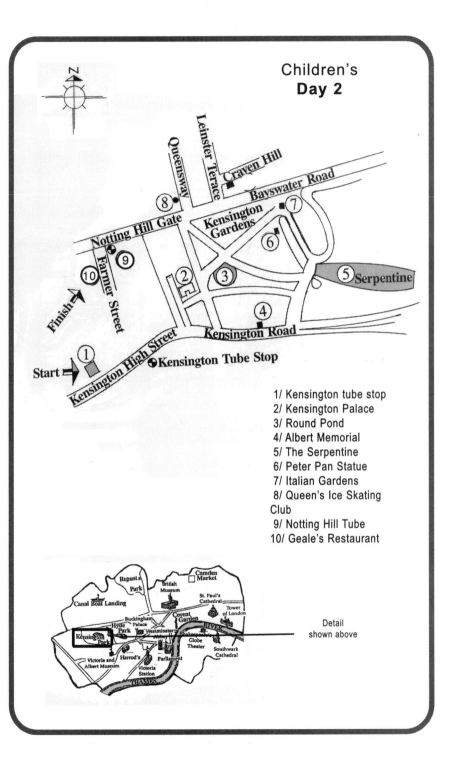

Children's
Day 2

N

Leinster Terrace

Queensway

Craven Hill

Bayswater Road

⑧

Notting Hill Gate

Kensington Gardens

⑦

⑥

⑨

⑤ Serpentine

Farmer Street

⑩

②

③

⑤ Serpentine

④

Finish

Start ➡ ①

Kensington High Street

Kensington Road

⊕ Kensington Tube Stop

1/ Kensington tube stop
2/ Kensington Palace
3/ Round Pond
4/ Albert Memorial
5/ The Serpentine
6/ Peter Pan Statue
7/ Italian Gardens
8/ Queen's Ice Skating Club
9/ Notting Hill Tube
10/ Geale's Restaurant

Regent's Park

Camden Market

British Museum

Canal Boat Landing

St. Paul's Cathedral

Tower of London

Buckingham Palace

Covent Garden

Kensington Park

Hyde Park

Westminster Abbey

RIVER

Globe Theater

Southwark Cathedral

Victoria and Albert Museum

Harrod's

Parliament

Victoria Station

THAMES

Detail
shown above

MORNING

A s you walk east along Kensington High Street to
Kensington Park, notice a big McDonald's directly
across the street. It is filled with chandeliers, mirrors,
plantings and comfortable seating, if you want a cup of
coffee or a roll at this point.

Walk up to the park and the Broad Walk which will
take you to **Kensington Palace** which opens at 10 a.m. to
6 p.m., March to October; 10 a.m. to 5 p.m., November to
February. Admission about $16 for adults; $12 for seniors
and $10 for children. They also have a family rate.

In 1689, architect Christopher Wren was asked to
design this country house for the royal family. Of particular interest to young people is **Queen Victoria's bedroom**
with her toys. Victoria lived here when she was princess
and learned of her accession to the throne, at the death of
William IV, in this room. Also notice the ivory throne and
footstool in the King's Council Chamber, a gift from the
Maharajah of Travancore. My favorite room is the
Presence Chamber with its painted ceiling, Grinling
Gibbons carvings around the fireplace and a throne.

② Directly in front of the palace is the **Round Pond**,
where little yachtsmen sail their boats. This is a very big
piece of water to be called a pond. If you happen to be
here on a Sunday, you will see some of the great kite flyers of the country. Just wander through this wonderful
park.

③ The exotic and ornate **Albert Memorial**, built by
Queen Victoria for her beloved spouse, is at the south
④ edge of the park. **The Serpentine**, the lake which snakes
through the park, separates Kensington Gardens from
Hyde Park.

NOON

A t the center of the park, you will come to the bridge
spanning the lake. To the right of the bridge (with the
palace to your back) you will see a restaurant, a bathing

pavilion and bath houses where you can change clothes for a **quick swim** in the lake.

Nearby is the Serpentine gallery with changing exhibitions of contemporary art. Stop for lunch at this point. There is an **inexpensive cafe** in the restaurant building.

AFTERNOON

AFTER LUNCH and swimming, walk north along the path on the edge of the **Serpentine** to see the **Peter Pan** statue and further on, the **Italian Gardens** with its fountains. If you have smaller children, walk back to the west end of the park to the children's playground. Exit the park and you will be on Bayswater Road. Cross Bayswater and walk to Queensway.

If you walk north on Queensway you will come to the **Queen's Ice Skating Club** on your left, the only indoors skating rink in central London. You can **rent skates** and have a twirl on the ice. Even if you don't want to skate, stop in and watch for a few minutes. I love this rink with its crepe paper flowers, buntings and turn-of-the-century decor. It is more like a ballroom than an ice rink.

EVENING

THIS IS a good time to stop and eat. From the Queensway tube stop, go one station to **Notting Hill** ⑨ **Tube** to have supper at **Geale's Restaurant**, one of the ⑩ best and oldest fish and chips places in London.

As you leave the tube station, turn left and walk a few steps to what looks like an alley, but is Farmer Street. Turn left and Geale's restaurant is a short block away. It has been a family owned business for nearly 50 years. Check the specials of the day; for example, mushroom soup, fish and chips and apple crumble (sort of like our apple crisp but better.) Priced at about $5. Good and inexpensive.

Tonight would be a good evening to cab to

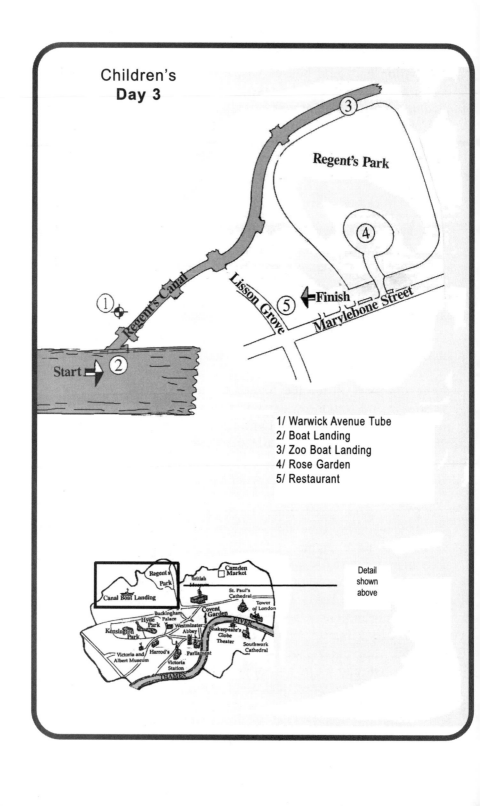

Children's
Day 3

Regent's Park

Regent's Canal

Lisson Grove

Finish

Marylebone Street

Start

1/ Warwick Avenue Tube
2/ Boat Landing
3/ Zoo Boat Landing
4/ Rose Garden
5/ Restaurant

Regent's Park
British Museum
Camden Market
St. Paul's Cathedral
Canal Boat Landing
Tower of London
Buckingham Palace
Covent Garden
Hyde Park
Westminster Abbey
Shakespeare's Globe Theater
Kensington Park
Southwark Cathedral
Victoria and Albert Museum
Harrod's
Parliament
Victoria Station
THAMES
RIVER

Detail
shown
above

Westminster pier and take a **trip up the Thames** to see the city illuminated. Your children will love the boats, the river and the lighted city - and so will you.

DAY 3

Highlights: Regent's Canal, London Zoo, Madame Tussaud's Wax Museum and the London Planetarium.

Reservations: No reservations necessary at any of the restaurants recommended in this chapter. Regent's Canal water-buses. For information telephone(020)7482 2660. Performance at the open air theatre in Regent's Park. For information, telephone 020/7486-2431.

MORNING

TODAY you will explore a curious mixture of London's pleasures - a canal boat trip, pandas from China, wax-work effigies, and a laser show.

Start the day with a **boat ride**. This would not be surprising in Venice or Amsterdam, but most people do not think of canals in London. Regents Canal was built in 1820 to join the Grand Union Canal with the Thames River at Limehouse, and it is wonderful.

Tube to **Warwick Avenue Tube stop** or take a cab to ① Little Venice, just off Blomfield Road, to the **Boat Landing** where the canal boats leave between 10 a.m. and ② 4:45 p.m.

Take one of the water buses from the pier to the Zoo Boat Landing at London Zoo in **Regent's Park**. Get the ③ ticket which includes admission to the zoo since that is your destination this morning.

This is a most unusual ride and the children and you will love seeing the houseboats that dock along the canal with their decorations of castles and roses.

G et off the boat at the **zoo landing**. You will be a short distance from an entrance to the zoo. Just follow the signs. **The London Zoo** is open daily 10 a.m. to 4 p.m.

This is the world's oldest zoo, open to the public in 1847. It was the brainchild of Sir Stamford Raffles, the famous Raffles, founder of Singapore. The zoo has grown from the original 5 acres to 36 acres, with 8,000 animals representing more than 1,160 species. In 1999 the zoo opened a new Conservation Centre to display the the wide variety of life on our planet. Stop at the entrance to get current information and a map.

Hopefully, the children's zoo and farm and Discovery Center will be open during your visit. Other areas to check are the 80-foot-high Snowdon Aviary with its more than 150 birds, the Great Apes Breeding Colony and the lion terrace.

NOON

S everal restaurants are located in or near the zoo. After lunch, leave the zoo to walk across Regent's Park.

Take any walk across the park; they will all lead you to Chester Road where you will turn right to arrive at **Queen Mary's Gardens**, the famous rose gardens and the ⑤ open air theater. The walk through the roses and over the little Japanese bridges, the lake and the pools will fascinate all of you.

A **restaurant and tea house** are near the rose garden. ④ If you did not eat in the restaurant at the zoo, this might be a good time for lunch.

AFTERNOON

L EAVE FROM the main entrance to Regent's Park, walk straight ahead to Marylebone Road, turn right and you will arrive at **Madame Tussaud's** famous waxwork museum.

The **London Planetarium** is next door; one ticket will admit you to both places.

Madame Tussaud's is open daily from 10 a.m. to 6 p.m. (5:30 p.m. October through March). The Planetarium is open 10 a.m. to 5 p.m. daily. There are often long lines of people waiting to get in, particularly in the summer.

Call in advance to avoid the long lines. 0870/400-3000. Admission is about $24 for adults, $17 for children. Children under 5 are free. There is a fast pick up desk near the entrance.

The figures and tableaux include entertainers and heroes, the royals in the Grand Hall, historical and fictional tableaux, and finally, the amazing Battle of Trafalgar.

Next door at the **Planetarium,** you will find the Astronomers Gallery on the ground floor and a one-half hour Star Show on the second floor.

EVENING

DEPENDING on your time (I cannot guess how much time you will spend in the zoo or other attractions) you are probably hungry again. Walk west on Marylebone Road to Lisson Grove, turn right to number 33 Lisson Grove to find the **Sea Shell Fish Bar.** This fish and chips place is very popular. You may even see some Rolls Royces waiting in front. You can either eat on the premises or take away to picnic.

After supper you may want to return to the Planetarium for the laser show or to Regent's Park for a performance in the **outdoor theatre.** Or both.

IN THREE SHORT DAYS you and your children have tasted many of the pleasures of London, just enough to want to savor more.

Additional suggestions: The **Unicorn Theatre** for Children, situated in the heart of London's theater district in the West End, is the only theater just for children. Founded in 1947 it presents a season of plays for 4 to 12-year-olds from September to June. 6 - 7 Great Newport

Street. Telephone (0171) 379 -3280. Show times:
September - June, Saturdays 11 a.m. and 2:30 p.m.;
Sundays and holidays, 2:30 p.m. Tube: Leicester Square.

And finally, rainy day alternatives:

S INCE A GOOD SHARE of the foregoing three days depend
on reasonably good weather, if you have a rainy morning or afternoon, go to the **British Museum.** (Tottenham
Court Road tube stop).

There are thousands of interesting things to see. The
great sculptures are on the main floor along with the Elgin
Marbles. Your children will probably be entranced with
the Egyptian galleries on the second floor with their
extensive display of mummies and mummy cases.

Or you could take them to my favorite: The
Mildenhall Treasure. This is a collection of gorgeous
Roman silver pieces...many of them big pieces..the greatest treasure ever found in the British Isles. It was found
by a farmer plowing up four or five acres for a neighbor.
Roald Dahl, the writer of many famous children's books
including *James and the Giant Peach* wrote a book about
this extraordinary event. It is titled *The Mildenhall
Treasure* and is for sale in the marvelous museum shop.

L ONDON is a wonderful place for children and for their
grown-up companions. These three days can be an
introduction to a lifetime love affair with this ageless city.

One Extra Special Event which can take hours or an
entire day. A visit to the **London Eye.** I call it a Ferris
wheel, but it is much more sophisticated than any Ferris
wheel I ever saw.

This was one of Great Britain's gifts in recognition of
The Millennium. It is the world's largest wheel, measur-
ing some 450 feet high. On a clear day you can see 25
miles around London. The 32 enclosed "pods" make a
complete round trip in about half an hour

The Eye is located in the Jubilee Gardens, near the

new pedestrian Hungerford footbridge. It is not hard to find. It would be liking missing the Eiffel Tower in Paris.

You can stand in line for tickets, but my advice is to get them in advance. For information and tickets call 0870 443 9185. There will be a booking fee, but I think it beats standing in line. Admission is about $20 for adults; $18 for seniors and $10 for children. It operates from 9 in the morning until about 10 p.m.

Since it is so difficult to estimate the time this excursion would take, I have added it as a very special bonus...for a clear, sunny day.

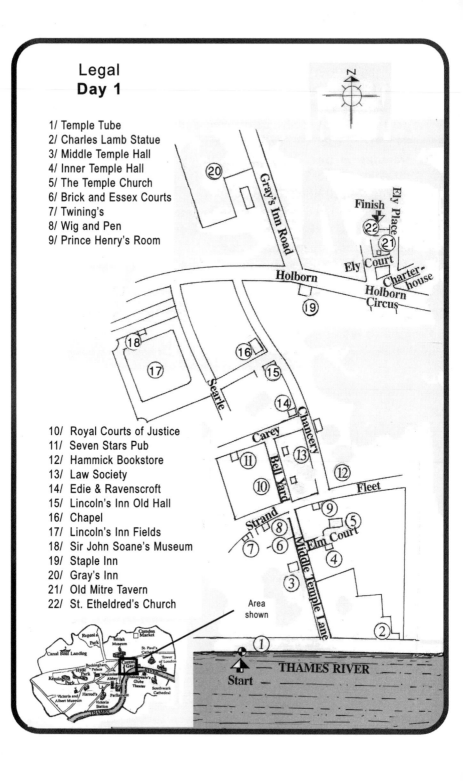

Legal
Day 1

1/ Temple Tube
2/ Charles Lamb Statue
3/ Middle Temple Hall
4/ Inner Temple Hall
5/ The Temple Church
6/ Brick and Essex Courts
7/ Twining's
8/ Wig and Pen
9/ Prince Henry's Room

10/ Royal Courts of Justice
11/ Seven Stars Pub
12/ Hammick Bookstore
13/ Law Society
14/ Edie & Ravenscroft
15/ Lincoln's Inn Old Hall
16/ Chapel
17/ Lincoln's Inn Fields
18/ Sir John Soane's Museum
19/ Staple Inn
20/ Gray's Inn
21/ Old Mitre Tavern
22/ St. Etheldred's Church

Gray's Inn Road

Finish
Ely Place
Ely Court
Charter-house
Holborn
Holborn Circus

Searle
Chancery
Carey
Bell Yard
Fleet
Strand
Elm Court
Middle Temple Lane

Area shown

Start — THAMES RIVER

LEGAL
LONDON

You don't need to be a lawyer
to be fascinated with this side of London

LEGAL LONDON is of interest to many more people than
just lawyers. The historical documents and buildings,
the ceremonial procedures attending the administration of
justice, and the unusual spaces housing and surrounding
these activities are fascinating to any visitor to this city.

The following three days will take you to the squares
of the Inns of Court; to the visitor's galleries in the Old
Bailey; to the magnificent Houses of Parliament; and to
some of the social spots filled with the men and women
who make and administer the law in London.

DAY 1

Highlights: Inns of Court, Royal Courts of Justice,
Public Record Office, Sir John Soane's Museum and
Staple Inn.

Reservations: Dinner at The Ivy, West Street.
Telephone 020 7240 9333.

Theatre reservations at St. Martin Theatre. Telephone:
020 7836-1443.

THE FOUR existing **Inns of Court:** the Middle and Inner Temple, Lincoln's Inn, and Gray's Inn were formed in the Middle Ages and aptly called inns because their original purpose was to give lodging to students of the law.

They began to train barristers and solicitors to replace the clergy, which stopped practicing in the courts of justice during the 13th century. Incidentally, barristers are the lawyers who plead in the higher courts; solicitors are the lawyers who research and brief barristers on their client's cases.

Today the Inns of Courts house few law students, but they do provide offices for many lawyers. (I will use the American word for members of the legal profession). They also offer lectures, provide law libraries and examine candidates for admission to the bar. In order to become a member of the bar, a student must be admitted, by examination, to one of these Inns of Court.

Some of the ancient and quiet squares and gardens which surround these old buildings are open to the public for walking and looking. Others are open only to members of the Inn and their guests. Some of the buildings, such as the chapels, are open to the public, others only to members. Only Lincoln's Inn is closed on the weekend.

MORNING

①   Start the day from the **Temple tube stop** about 9:30 a.m. Go east along the Embankment to a small walkway on your left, the Middle Temple Lane. Walk up the lane to
② **Middle Temple Hall,** dating from 1573. It may be visited only by appointment. Write Treasury Office, Middle Temple, London EC4Y9AT or telephone 020 7353-5355 for appointment. Inner Temple Hall is open these same hours. Despite announced opening times, the buildings are often closed for special occasions and always closed from noon to 3 p.m. There is no guarantee they will be open.

The **Middle Temple Hall** was heavily damaged in World War II bombing, but has been restored. Particularly

note the unusual double hammerbeam roof. One of the
stained glass windows features two of the Inn's readers
(students of the law), Mr.Jekyll and Mr. Hyde. You now
know where Mr. Stevenson found the names for his book.
The 16th century carved screen at the east end of the hall
was completely shattered by a bomb and carefully put
back together like a gigantic jigsaw puzzle.

Walk Middle Temple Lane a few steps to Elm Court
and **Temple Church of St. Mary.** The church, built by the ⑤
Knights Templars between 1160 and 1185 as a copy of the
Church of Holy Sepulcher in Jerusalem, is the most
important round church in England. It serves both the
Inner and Middle Temples. (Open Wed. to Sat. 11 a.m. to
4 p.m.; Sun 1 to 4 p.m.

To ENTER, turn the metal ring to open the door. The first
time I was there, I pulled and pushed and thought it
was closed. Just turn the ring and it will open easily.

Of particular interest are the medieval effigies of
knights, perhaps the oldest-known English statues.
Lawyers used to wait for their clients here in the Round.

Walk around the grounds of both these Inns of Courts
to feel the air of contemplation and learning, to watch the
barristers in their wigs and robes striding through the gardens and to remember the men who lived and studied here:
Charles Lamb; Oliver Goldsmith; the famous jurist
Blackstone, who complained about Goldsmith's noises;
and Dr. Johnson and Thackeray.

If you walk near the river, you may see the memorial
fountain honoring Charles Lamb with the charming
inscription, *Lawyers were children once.* I urge you not to
hurry. This is a special and serene place.

WALK UP Middle Temple Lane to **Brick Court** and ⑥
Essex Court, turn left and walk beneath overhang-
ing sections of buildings. Another reminder to look overhead.

At the far end of Essex Court you will find a glass

door. Open it and walk through the glass-domed hallway. You will emerge on the Strand, number 222 Strand to be exact, just opposite the Royal Courts of Justice. It is always a shock to leave the quiet precincts of the Temple courts and spill out on noisy, busy Fleet Street.

(10) WALK ACROSS to the impressive **Royal Courts of Justice** building (1874-82). The civil cases, which used to be heard in Westminster, are now heard in the 20 courtrooms in this building. It is open Monday to Friday from 9 a.m. to 4:30 p.m. The information desk will provide a guide to the building.

Wander through the Great Hall, with its mosaic pavement, and visit the exhibition of legal costumes in a room near the main entrance. Save your court visits for the Old Bailey Criminal Courts.

NOON

(8) BY NOW it should be time to think of eating. Several choices: Just across the street from the Royal Courts is the **Wig and Pen Club.** Incidentally, it is just about here that Fleet Street becomes Strand Street. This happens all the time in London and is terribly confusing for the visitor but be assured it is the same street, just a different name.

The Wig and Pen is a private club, primarily filled with lawyers and journalists, but foreign visitors can receive immediate free temporary membership by just asking for one. The food is good; the decor fascinating and it is an enchanting place to eat. Lots of little cubby hole rooms as well as larger areas, plus a lounge and tiny bathrooms.

The Wig and Pen building was the only one in the Strand to survive the Great Fire of London in 1666...it was built on Roman ruins in 1625. It still has the original wooden suspended staircase, believed to be the only one of its kind still in existence anywhere in the world.

Lunch is served from 12:30 p.m. to 6 p.m.; dinner at 6 p.m. There is also a luncheon bar with hot and cold snacks, plus low calorie dishes for people in a hurry or just watching their waistline.

Another choice for lunch: Walk up Bell Yard along the side of the Royal Courts of Justice to Carey Street, turn left to the **Seven Stars Pub**, a lawyer's hangout, with legal cartoons on the walls. This pub celebrated its 400th birthday in 2001.

Notice two other buildings on the Strand/Fleet Street. **Twinings tea shop**, just west of the Wig and Pen, was established in 1716. However, only the doorway survives from the original building. The store is at best 10 feet wide.

At number 17 Fleet Street, note **Prince Henry's Room**. Nobody is exactly sure about the history of this place. It was probably not connected with royalty, but its upstairs tavern room with its Jacobean paneling and its mementos from Samuel Pepys is worth a look. Open 11 a.m. to 2 p.m., Monday - Saturday. Even if you don't care about Mr. Pepys, the original stained glass and Jacobean ceilings are more worth your time.

AFTERNOON

W̲ALK TO Chancery Lane to the next Inn of Court, Lincoln's Inn. The law bookstore, **Hammick**, is nearby at number 191/192 Fleet St., established in 1799.

Up Chancery Lane to number 94 and the shop, **Ede & Ravenscroft**. They have been purveying gowns and wigs since 1693. Even if you are not interested in buying a wig or robe, stop in to see their display of ceremonial garments.

Continue up Chancery Lane to the Gatehouse of 1521, which will admit you to **Lincoln's Inn**. The Inn's old buildings, **Old Hall** and the Chapel, are just ahead. The Old Hall is open when not in use. If it is closed, inquire at the nearby porter's office. He may be willing to take you

on a tour through the hall and the chapel. Just tip him.
They are both fascinating buildings.

THE OLD HALL is the finest building in the Inn with its
scissor roof beams, stained glass and the huge
Hogarth painting *Paul Before Felix* hanging in the same
place almost continuously since 1748.

(16)   As you walk toward the **Chapel,** you will walk
through an Undercroft/crypt at ground level. The chapel
stands on pillars above it. Its carved pillars and ceiling
are quite extraordinary. The Chapel is usually open
Monday to Friday, noon to 2 p.m. Note the limited open
hours.

The Chapel was built from 1619 to 1623 to replace a
former chapel which had become 'ruinous', as they say,
and was too small. The poet and churchman, **John Donne**,
laid the cornerstone and preached the opening sermon.
The Spanish chapel bell tolls curfew at 9 p.m. each night
and also tolls the news of the death of a member of the
inn. It may be from this custom that Donne found the
source for his famous words: "Never send to know for
whom the bell tolls; it tolls for thee."

The great stained glass window on the east contains
the arms of the 228 Treasurers of the Society from 1680-
1908. The arms of Treasurers from 1909 to 1962 are in the
east window on the north side and those from 1963
onwards are in the west window.

(17)   LINCOLN'S INN FIELDS are just beyond the Inns of
Court. This is the largest square in central London,
designed by Inigo Jones, and the home for many of the
famous. It was also the location for the pillory where Lord
William Russell was executed.

Walk around the square and admire the lovely old
homes and medical buildings. At this point I am com-
pelled to add a side trip which has nothing to do with law
or lawyers, but since it and you are both here, I cannot let
you walk past it.

At No. 13 on the square you will find the most unusual museum in London, **Sir John Soane's Museum**. Soane, architect for the Bank of England, left his home and collections to the city with the stipulation they could not be changed in any way. It is his private house, just as he lived in it. (Open 10 a.m. to 5 p.m. Tuesday through Saturday).

I do not know how to describe this eclectic collection, which ranges from the sarcophagus of Seti I to paintings by Watteau and Canaletto. The Picture Room contains two famous series of paintings by William Hogarth: *The Election* and *The Rake's Progress*.

Ask the guard to show you the folding storage arrangements for these paintings. It is not just the collections, but the house and the way things are displayed that make a visit so fascinating. The use of mirrors, recessed ceilings and walls, angled windows, half flights, arched ceilings and all manner of strange and disorienting architectural arrangements turn this house into a strange and magical experience.

IT IS probably now about 3 or 3:30 p.m. Walk up to Holborn Street, cross over and quickly walk through **Gray's Inn of Court**. I find this the least interesting Inn of Court, but the gardens are lovely, especially the one laid out by philosopher Sir Francis Bacon, which contains his statue.

Walk on down Holborn (east) to **Staple Inn** on your right. This was part of the Chancery Inn and was both an inn and a market place for wool traders, known as 'staplers', hence the name. It is the only remaining half-timbered terrace in London. Be sure to walk into the quiet inner court.

You probably need to sit down at this point and have some sustenance. Walk west on Holborn to Holborn Circus, angle off on Charterhouse to Ely Place and look for the **Old Mitre Tavern.** You will have to search for an ornate gaslamp and a very little sign, then worm your way down the alley to one of the smallest pubs in London. It dates from 1546. The pub consists of a couple of tiny rooms and an outdoor patio for summer, but I think you will find it endearing.

If you have any energy left, you can look at the 18th century houses on Ely Place and the beautiful St. (22) **Etheldreda** Church, built about 1300, Britain's oldest existing Catholic church.

EVENING

G o back to your hotel for a rest, if it is convenient, and then on to the theatre. *The Mousetrap* by Agatha Christie playing at the St. Martin Theatre for more than three decades, might be an appropriate, if corny, selection for tonight. The best thing about this choice is that right across the way, on little West Street, is my favorite restaurant again, **The Ivy**.

Tomorrow you will visit the courts at the Old Bailey and see some of the lawyers at work who studied in the great Inns of Court you visited this morning.

Gresham

Lothbury

Threadneedle

King

Prince

Poultry

Cornhill

Leadenhall

Watling

Gracechurch

King William

Eastcheap

Great
Tower

Byward

RIVER

Finish

N

Area shown
in large map

Regent's
Park

Camden
Market

British
Museum

St. Paul's
Cathedral

Canal Boat Landing

Tower
of London

Buckingham
Palace

Covent
Garden

Hyde
Park

Westminster
Abbey

RIVER

Kensington
Park

Shakespeare's
Globe
Theater

Southwark
Cathedral

Victoria and
Albert Museum

Harrod's

Parliament

Victoria
Station

THAMES

1/ Barbican Tube
2/ Charterhouse Square
3/ Smithfield Market
4/ St. Bartholomew's Church
5/ "Fat Boy" Statue
6/ St. Sepulchre's Church
7/ Old Bailey
8/ Viaduct Tavern
9/ St. Paul's Cathedral
10/ Guildhall
11/ Bank of England
12/ Stock Exchange
13/ Royal Exchange
14/ Leadenhall Market
15/ Monument
16/ Tower of London

DAY 2

Highlights: Old Bailey Criminal Courts, Guildhall, Bank of England, and the Tower of London. Reservations: Dinner at the Gay Hussar, 2 Greek Street. Telephone: 020 7437-4631.

MORNING

A REMINDER: Do not take a camera with you today or you will not be admitted to any of the Central Criminal Court buildings. It is just too easy to hide an explosive device in a camera case.They make no exceptions.

This morning, you will start your day just east of where you drank your beer yesterday afternoon. You are headed for the **Old Bailey Criminal Court** at 10:30 a.m., but because you will be in the neighborhood, I suggest an early morning start to visit one of the city's oldest and most fascinating districts.

You can stay in bed and cab to the Old Bailey at 10:30 a.m, but I think you will miss an exciting, though bloody, morning.

 TAKE THE TUBE to the **Barbican Tube** stop or cab to Smithfield Market. Walk down either **Charterhouse** or West Smithfield /Long Lane Street to the market. **Smithfield Market's** 10 acres are now the largest meat market in the world.

Smithfield, meaning smooth field, was the most important cloth fair in England during the Middle Ages. It was a horse and cattle market from 1150 to 1855; the main place of execution in the 12th century, and the site of the great St. Bartholomew's Fair from the 1100's until 1840. The market is its busiest between the hours of 4 and 9 a.m.

Go early and wander around the market to watch the burly porters cart the enormous slabs of meat on carts around the marketplace.

Believe me, if you get in their way, they will let you

know. It is an incredible and amazing sight. It is not as
bloody as it used to be now that most of the meat is in
gauze wrapping, but you might be somewhat tempted to
think about vegetarianism.

Incidentally, some of the local pubs (exempt from the
regular opening hours) can provide a good breakfast.

WALK TO the Smithfield green and about a half a block
on your left you will find the arched entrance to the
little garden which will lead you to **St. Bartholomew the**   ④
Great Church, built in 1123, the oldest church still standing in London. It was built by courtier Rahere, one of
Henry I's court. He began his life as something of a court
jester and playboy, but following the death of Henry's
beloved son and Rahere's own severe illness, he vowed to
build a great church and he did.

The building is in need of renovation, but I find it perhaps the most spiritual and wonderful church in London. I
love to come here for Sunday services with its small con-
gregation and lovely choir.

Note the great arches reminiscent of both Roman and
Norman styles and the decorated tomb of Rahere.

Walk behind the altar to the **Lady Chapel** to see the
location of what was once a printing press where
Benjamin Franklin was employed. Hogarth, the artist, was
baptized at the medieval font. Be sure to notice the
needlepoint kneeling bench with its animals, fish and
birds of the earth just behind the altar railing.

AS YOU LEAVE the church walk to your left down
Giltspur Street. Look for little Cock Lane on your
right. At the corner of these two streets, inserted in the
wall above eye level, you will see the statue of what is
known as the **Fat Boy.**   ⑤

The little gold boy stands shivering in the morning air.
Legend, if not fact, says this marks the location where the
Great Fire,1666, stopped. The lane itself was licensed for
prostitution during medieval days.

Continue down Giltspur Street to Newgate. On your
⑥ right is **St. Sepulchre's Church.**

⑦ To your left and straight ahead are the **Central
Criminal Courts of London (Old Bailey).** It should be
about 10:30 a.m. and time for the public to be admitted to
the galleries.

IF YOU WALK straight down what is now Old Bailey, you
will come to the new court buildings. I suggest you turn
left and walk east on Newgate Street. As you walk along
the side of the old **Old Bailey,** look carefully for *a door, a
small marker and a bell.* It is not particularly well marked.

Ring the bell. A guard will let you in and direct you to
the steps which take you to the visitors galleries. Bailiffs
sit either right outside each courtroom, or immediately
inside the door, and will tell you whether there is room for
you in the gallery. Courts number 1 and 2 usually handle
the more important trials. Incidentally, afternoon sessions
begin about 2 p.m. Sit in the front row if possible. Of all
the things I love to do in London, this is my favorite.

I will never forget the first time I climbed those steps,
walked into the galleries, sat down and looked down into
that old courtroom: I suddenly felt as though I had fallen
back two hundred years in time to see the judge, in his
robes beneath the great seal, the barristers in their wigs
and robes, and the prisoner in the dock. As I listened to all
the legal and stilted words, the formality of presentation
washed over me, and I was back with Dickens and
Shakespeare and all the people who have written or taught
me about law, justice, the Magna Carta and democracy. I
found it irresistible and almost impossible to leave.

On opening day, the judges still carry posies to court
to ward off fever, and herbs are strewn around the room to
cover the terrible smells from the infamous Newgate
prison, once located on the site of the old Old Bailey.
Think about the figure of Justice which stands on the top
of the building with its scales, but without a blindfold;
and about St. Sepulchre's Church across the street, where

the hand bell, which used to ring at midnight outside prisoner's cells to announce the day of their execution, is on
view but no longer in use.

Then you pay attention to the case in court today,
probably a robbery or assault, much like our own, but with
a legal style and presentation so different. I defy you to
stay only five minutes.

NOON

A S YOU LEAVE the old building, cross Newgate Street to
the **Viaduct Tavern** at 126 Newgate. This old pub
was established in 1869 opposite what was then Newgate
Prison and is now the Old Bailey. Look at the old paintings and mirrors. Many years ago they lodged debtors in
cells still located in this pub's basement. Sometimes the
proprietor will walk you down to these old cells.

AFTERNOON

T HIS AFTERNOON you are going to visit **The City,** the
square mile which encompasses the financial district
of London and includes the great Guildhall. You will also
walk past the Bank of England on your way to the historic
Tower of London.

Walk up west on Newgate Street, turn left on Old
Bailey to Ludgate Hill, turn left, walk past and around **St.**
Paul's Cathedral. Visit it if you are so inclined. Walk
behind the cathedral to Watling Street, the oldest street in
London.

Turn left on Queen Street which becomes King Street
and finally Guildhall Yard just in front of the **Guildhall,**
seat of municipal government for London. The Great Hall
is open Monday through Saturday 10 a.m. to 5 p.m. The
Hall was used for municipal meetings, the election of the
Lord Mayor and sheriffs of London and state banquets.
Earlier it was used for important trials. The trials are listed on a plaque on the wall. A short visit will suffice here.

Incidentally a new home for the Greater London

Authority (City Hall), designed by architect Norman Foster, was completed in 2001. It is located on the south side of the Thames, almost opposite the Tower of London.

(11) Walk east on Gresham Street, turn right on Prince's Street to the **Bank of England** on Threadneedle Street. Remember *The Old Lady of Threadneedle*, the name for the Bank of England?

In 1989, the Bank of England opened its doors to the public for the first time. Visitors are now permitted to tour the building and its new museum, which features a reconstruction of the world's first stock office and an exhibition of the bank's original charter, gold bars and bank notes. A videotape program explaining the workings of the bank and its role in the financial world are shown to visitors. Admission is free.

(13) The **Royal Exchange** across the street is usually open for temporary exhibitions. Note the glass-roofed courtyard with its unusual pavement and the historical wall-

(12) panel paintings. The **Stock Exchange** visitor's gallery, just beyond the bank on Threadneedle Street, is closed to the public.

(15)
(14) Walk down Gracechurch Street past the glass enclosed **Leadenhall Market** to the **Monument.** This marks the approximate spot where the Great Fire (1666) began. The monument is 202 feet high; the spot where the fire actually started on Pudding Lane is exactly 202 feet from this spot.

Turn left on Eastcheap, which becomes Great Tower Street, and then Byward Street and you will be at the

(16) **Tower of London.** It seems appropriate to end this day of sightseeing at the Tower which held prisoners as a result of some of the most famous trials in London. Of particular interest on this tour are the **White Tower**, where Sir Walter Raleigh spent 13 years during his second imprisonment; Byward Tower, which was the prison for Sir Thomas More and Princess Elizabeth; and Tower Green,

where a scaffold was erected. Anne Boleyn and Catherine Howard, two of Henry VIII's wives, were executed here along with Lady Jane Grey and the Earl of Essex.

EVENING

Take a cab back to your hotel and rest. Tonight you might want to try a Hungarian restaurant which has always attracted lawyers, politicians and literary people, the **Gay Hussar** at 2 Greek Street in Soho. Dinner for two should be moderate in price. If you feel like it, walk around Soho after dinner; it is lively with strip shows and sex shops.

DAY 3

Highlights: Houses of Parliament, Westminster Abbey and the Chapter House, Number 10 Downing Street, and Buckingham Palace.

Reservations: Lunch at Shepherd's restaurant, Marsham Court, Marsham Street. Telephone 020 7834-9552. Dinner at Rules restaurant, 35 Maiden Lane. Telephone 020 7836-5314. Reservations for theatre tickets to see the Royal Shakespeare Company. Check newspapers or magazines for information concerning performance schedules.

MORNING

This morning's tour of the **Houses of Parliament** is predicated on a simple given: that they are open. There is absolutely no way of knowing whether they will be open or closed, or what open hours may be in effect. It all depends on the political climate, when or if the parliamentary bodies are in session and a number of other variables. You must check on open times when you arrive. Read the newspapers or ask at your hotel.

Westminster Tube stop is closest to the Houses of Parliament, or cab there. If you take the tube, climb the

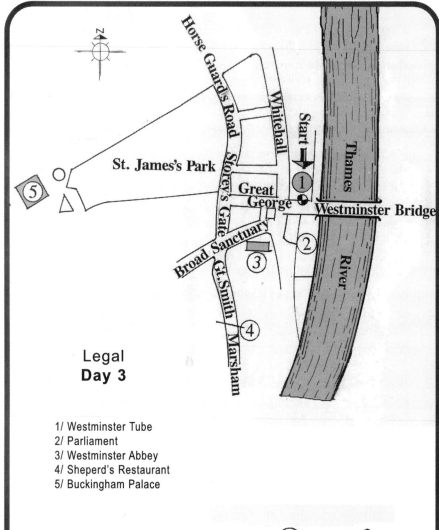

Legal
Day 3

1/ Westminster Tube
2/ Parliament
3/ Westminster Abbey
4/ Sheperd's Restaurant
5/ Buckingham Palace

Area
shown
above

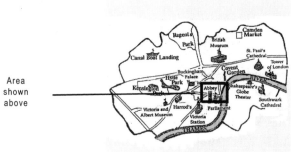

stairs and walk out on to Westminster Bridge for a look at the Houses of Parliament and Big Ben as well as the Thames.

You can take a guided tour or walk through the **Houses of Parliament** by yourself, which is more leisurely. I must admit that I like the tour because the guides are so smitten with the buildings and their history that they add a great deal to the experience. Everything that follows depends on the political climate of the time. Since the recent terrorist attacks around the world, many changes have been made regarding the public access to governmental buildings.

The **entrance** to Westminster Hall is from St. Stephen's porch; the entrance to the Houses of Parliament from the Victoria Tower.

The tour of Parliament begins as you walk up the Royal Staircase of the Norman Porch. On the right is the Queen's Robing Room. At the far end is Queen Victoria's chair of state.

Next is the 110-foot-long Royal Gallery with its lovely ceiling. The Prince's Chamber is the ante room to the House of Lords. The 80-foot-long Gothic **House of Lords,** which seats more than 1,000 peers, is too glorious to describe. You will stand in awe of this magnificently decorated chamber.

The Queen's throne is at the north end. In front of the throne is the Woolsack, an ordinary looking ottoman stuffed with wool from countries throughout the Commonwealth. It is a reminder that the wool trade once represented England's wealth.

THE PEERS' LOBBY, Robing Room and Library are usually not shown to visitors. The Peers' Corridor leads to the Central Lobby which is the division between the House of Lords and the House of Commons.

Pass through the Commons Corridor, lobby and library. On the north is the Churchill Arch.

The **House of Commons** was destroyed during an air

raid on May 10, 1941 and was rebuilt and reopened in 1950. 650 members sit on the green hide benches. The party in office sits to the right of the Speaker's chair. Two red lines between the benches form the boundary beyond which not one step may be taken during debate.

Historically, they are two sword lengths apart. A formal ceremony opens each day. Visitors in the gallery can get a copy of the day's agenda from a messenger.

RETURN TO the Central lobby.On the west is **St. Stephen's Hall** where Commons met from 1547-1834. St. Stephen's steps lead you to Westminster, one of the only parts of the medieval building still standing, built originally in 1097-9, and rebuilt after several fires. The hall is the great chamber of a royal palace, the meeting place of the Great Council, predecessor to Parliament and the Courts of Justice.

The chief court of English law sat here from the late 13th century to 1825, when the Royal Courts of Justice opened. Here Edward II was forced to abdicate in 1327; the pretender Perkin Warbeck was condemned to death in 1499; Sir Thomas More, the Earl of Essex and Guy Fawkes were tried; Oliver Cromwell was installed as protector in 1653; and coronation feasts were held. Be sure to notice the hammerbeam room with its 12 bays.

NOON

④ FOR LUNCH today, I suggest **Sheperd's** restaurant on Marsham Court, Marsham Street. Walk down The Broad Sanctuary to Great Smith Street, turn left. After crossing Great Peter Street you are on Marsham Street.

AFTERNOON

③ WALK BACK to **Westminster Abbey** to the **Chapter House**, which served, in 1257, as the meeting place for Parliament's predecessor, the Great Council, and later as the House of Commons. It is just behind the Abbey. Visit the Abbey if you will, following the plan in the Basic Three Days in London.

THIS AFTERNOON retrace your steps to the Houses of Parliament and turn left on Whitehall past the government buildings, Number 10 Downing Street, the horse guards and the Admiralty. Turn left and walk down the mall or through St. James's Park to **Buckingham Palace.** This is a good walk to remind you that the monarchy exists, perhaps without much real power today, but a reminder of its majestic history.

Walk through Buckingham Palace Gardens and down Halkin Street to **Belgrave Square.** Here you will find a number of handsome buildings housing the Norwegian, Saudi Arabia and German embassies. Surrounding streets contain a number of other embassy and official residences. Continue your walk through Belgravia until you arrive at Brompton Road and Harrod's great department store. You should be just in time for their famous 4 p.m. tea, which should hold you until supper, either before or after the theatre.

EVENING

TONIGHT try the **Royal Shakespeare Company.** With some kind of luck they might be doing the Merchant of Venice, but go see whatever they are doing. They will be guilty of doing it superbly. And sum up with dinner at Rules, 35 Maiden Lane,London's oldest restaurant (1798). You can eat things such as jugged hare or boiled beef and finish off with English trifle. Expensive.

LEGAL LONDON took you from Parliament to the Tower of London; from the lawyer's pubs to the Old Bailey. It was a long trip through history but a short three days of walking and sightseeing.

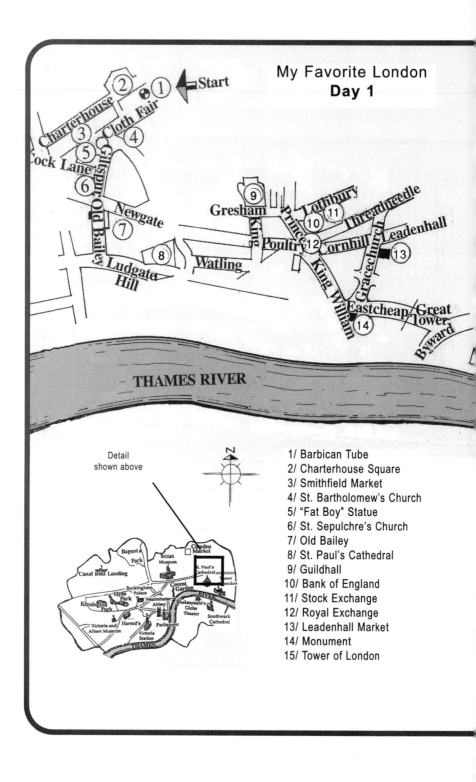

My Favorite London
Day 1

Start

Charterhouse · Cloth Fair · Cock Lane · Giltspur · Old Bailey · Newgate · Ludgate Hill · Watling · Gresham · King · Prince · Poultry · Lothbury · Cornhill · Threadneedle · Leadenhall · Gracechurch · King William · Eastcheap · Great Tower · Byward

THAMES RIVER

Detail
shown above

N

1/ Barbican Tube
2/ Charterhouse Square
3/ Smithfield Market
4/ St. Bartholomew's Church
5/ "Fat Boy" Statue
6/ St. Sepulchre's Church
7/ Old Bailey
8/ St. Paul's Cathedral
9/ Guildhall
10/ Bank of England
11/ Stock Exchange
12/ Royal Exchange
13/ Leadenhall Market
14/ Monument
15/ Tower of London

MY FAVORITE
THREE DAYS

The author picks her all-time
favorite things to see and do in London

IF I ONLY had three days to spend in London, I would have a very hard time picking and choosing where I would go and what I would see. I had to think about this for a long time and was actually surprised at some of the places I chose. Some were very easy and others were difficult. After all my advice to my readers, I thought this would be easy. But it wasn't.

DAY 1

Highlights: Smithfield Market, Old St. Batholomew's Church, Old Bailey Criminal Court, St. Paul's Cathedral, Leadenhall Market, St. Mary-at-the-Hill Church, and the Tower of London.

Reservations: Theatre tickets for the Royal Shakespeare Company at the Barbican Theatre. Telephone: 020/7638-8891.

MORNING

③ I WOULD START early at **Smithfield Market**, 8 a.m. even though it actually begins around 4 a.m.,much too early for me, and wander around the huge meat market. I still am not sure why this fascinates me so much, but it does. The site is so old and the market so bustling and alive that I find it exciting. This is the largest meat market in the world. I like what it is and what it was. Until 1840 the great St. Batholomew's Fair was here; England's famous cloth fair operated here during the Middle Ages; and in the 12th century it was a place of execution.

④   Down to **Old St. Bartholomew's Church** and around its damp and ancient aisles to visit Rahere's (founder of the church) tomb, its round arches and its 15th century font.

⑦   Then on to the old **Old Bailey Criminal Courts** for the opening at 10 a.m. Remember: no cameras, cellphones or tape recorders and no place to check them. The guards will tell you which pub or shop across the street is willing to check them.

    Nothing I ever do in London is quite so thrilling and awesome as sitting in one of the galleries in this old courthouse. Every time I suspect it will be more familiar and ordinary, but it never is. It is the best theatre in London and I never tire of looking at the robes and wigs and listening to the formal and stilted language of the barristers and judges and the street language of the defendants. It hasn't changed in hundreds of years, I am sure.

NOON

⑨ W ALK UP Ludgate Hill to **St. Paul's Cathedral** for a quick walk to the American Chapel and a visit with my old friend, John Donne, in his funeral shroud.

    Around to the back of the cathedral and a walk down Watling Street, the oldest street in London, and over to the
⑪ **Bank of England.** Then a wander through the triangle

where the **George and Vulture pub** is located and little lanes and alleys intersect. Stop for lunch.

AFTERNOON

Over to Gracechurch Street and a look in the **Leadenhall Market** and its meat and vegetable stands. Down Gracechurch Street to the **Monument** where the Great Fire started. And no, I will not climb its internal spiral staircase with its 311 steps.

Eastcheap Street to Lovat Lane and a stop in St. Mary-at-Hill Church and on to the **Tower of London** for a look around. No Jewel Tower this afternoon. Just a walk around and maybe a visit to the Chapel of St. John's in the White Tower.

Take a **boat** from **Tower Pier** to Westminster Pier and out on the bridge to see the Houses of Parliament, Big Ben and the Abbey. Perhaps a quick look in the Abbey if I have any strength left.

EVENING

Take a cab to the Barbican Theatre to see whatever the **Royal Shakespeare Company** is doing and a bite of supper after the theatre at one of the restaurants in the Barbican complex.

DAY 2

Highlights: Trafalgar Square, National Portrait Gallery, Charing Cross Road, Covent Garden, Regent's Park and the National Theatre.

Reservations: Theatre reservations for a production at the Royal National Theatre. Telephone for reservations: 020/7452-3400.

Reservations for lunch at The Ivy: 020-7836 4750.

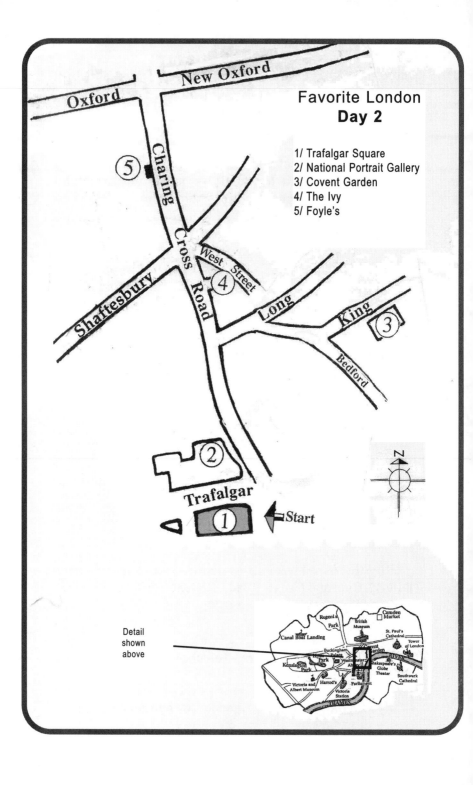

**Favorite London
Day 2**

1/ Trafalgar Square
2/ National Portrait Gallery
3/ Covent Garden
4/ The Ivy
5/ Foyle's

MORNING

S tart at **Trafalgar Square** this morning. To some, ①
Piccadilly Circus is the center of London, to others the
Bank of England in the center of The City. To me the center of London is Trafalgar Square with its crowds of
tourists, swarms of too-friendly pigeons and Landseer's
lions guarding the fountains. I love the views in every
direction.

To the **National Portrait Gallery** for a quick look. I ②
think if I had to pick just one museum that captures the
essence of this country, it would be this small gallery.
Actually it is not so small except in comparison to the
behemoths such as the British Museum and the Victoria
and Albert Museum. I always look at Richard III's sad
image, Henry VIII's enormous "cartoon", and the Bronte
sisters with the ghost of their brother looming over their
shoulders. Everybody important in English history is here.

Then up Charing Cross Road to Cecil and St. Martin's
Courts, Goodwin's Court and over to **Covent Garden.** All ③
those tiny little alleyways with their bow-windowed shops
give me the feeling of old London. Covent Garden is lively and largely renovated since the removal of the old market. But it still has lots of charm. I like to walk in the
damp shady garden leading to old St. Paul's Church and
wander around inside looking at the plaques.

Back to Charing Cross Road and up to the Cambridge
Circus, looking at the book stores. This is a chance to
stick my head in **84 Charing Cross**, the location of Helen
Hanff's beloved book. It is no longer a bookstore, but visitors to this "shrine" are welcome. A sign tells you, yes,
you are in the right place and to look around.

NOON

T URN ON West Street for lunch at **The Ivy.** This is my ④
favorite restaurant in London. I still remember the
first time I arrived for lunch: no reservations, slightly

damp from a long morning in the rain, dressed in slacks and my practical "walking" shoes ... and alone. I will never forget the way I was treated, like the Queen of England.

They hung up my wet coat, offered me an aperitif, commiserated about the weather and ushered me to a lovely table where I was smothered with care. I would like to think they always behave that way, but of course I cannot guarantee it.

This was also the site of my first encounter with "whitebait". They are often listed on London menus under Appetizers. They are a tiny fish, about the size of small goldfish, which are French fried and served in large quantities with lemon. They look exactly like deep fried gold fish and taste sort of like French fries. You just have to get over the strange sensation of eating little whole goldfish. They are very good.

AFTERNOON

⑤ AFTER LUNCH, back to Charing Cross to **Foyle's bookstore.** I know Foyle's is enormous, crowded, complicated and purchasing a book is almost impossible, but I love it. All the things other people find difficult, I find endearing. There is no explanation for some booklover's taste. If I happen to find a knowledgeable clerk, it can be heaven. Otherwise, I just wander around and almost always find treasures.

Then a cab to **Regent's Park** and to spend time in Queen Mary's rose garden. There is a nice restaurant and tearoom when I tire of wandering through the gardens, smelling the roses and crossing the little bridges.

EVENING

A play again this evening, probably at the Royal National Theatre. Afterward, a walk back across the new pedestrian bridge..the Hungerford Bridge.. to see the city lighted. It is an awesome and beautiful sight.

DAY 3

Highlights: Piccadilly Circus, Jermyn Street, Fortnum and Mason's, the Tate Gallery, Beauchamp Place and Kensington Gardens.

Reservations: Lunch reservations at the Tate Gallery Restaurant. Telephone: 020- 887-8825. Dinner reservations at Rules restaurant. Telephone: 020- 7836-5314.

MORNING

Today it's **Piccadilly Circus** and a walk down Jermyn ①
Street with all its old shops and their unforgettable smells. Paxton and Whithead's hams and cheeses greet you halfway down the block and the perfumer Floris is always enticing.

I don't smoke anymore, but Dunhill's tobacco shop fills the air with memories of earlier days and images of pipes and tweeds.

Fortnum and Mason's is a necessary stop. I must see ③
the fanciest grocery in town and its clerks in their tail coats. Even this early in the day I wouldn't bet against my having a soda on the mezzanine. They have the best bitter chocolate soda I ever tasted.

To St. James's Street and on to **St. James's Park.** ④
Wander around the park to see the folks stretched out in their canvas chairs and feed the exotic birds with scones from Fortnum's.

NOON

Probably time for lunch and where better than the **Tate Britain.** With luck I will have remembered to make a reservation. After lunch a visit to look at the Turners and hunt out my friend Atkinson-Grimshaw's misty paintings of harbors.

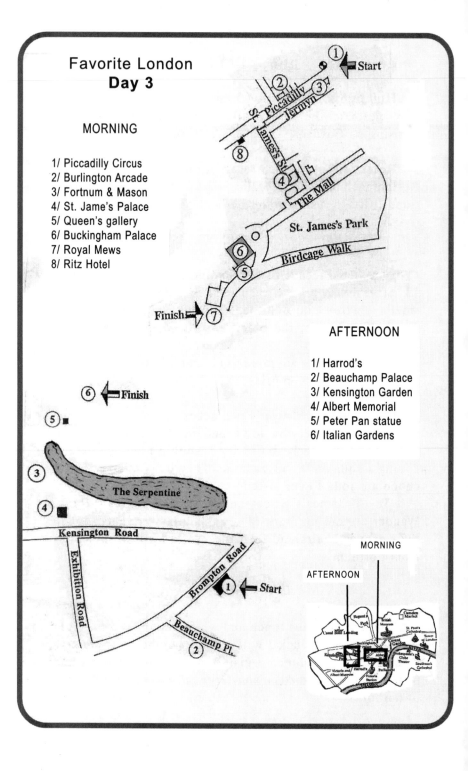

Favorite London
Day 3

MORNING

1/ Piccadilly Circus
2/ Burlington Arcade
3/ Fortnum & Mason
4/ St. Jame's Palace
5/ Queen's gallery
6/ Buckingham Palace
7/ Royal Mews
8/ Ritz Hotel

Start

① Piccadilly
② Jermyn
③
St. James's St.
⑧
④
The Mall
St. James's Park
⑥ Birdcage Walk
⑤
Finish ⑦

AFTERNOON

1/ Harrod's
2/ Beauchamp Palace
3/ Kensington Garden
4/ Albert Memorial
5/ Peter Pan statue
6/ Italian Gardens

⑥ Finish
⑤
③
The Serpentine
④
Kensington Road
Exhibition Road
Brompton Road
① Start
Beauchamp Pl.
②

MORNING
AFTERNOON

AFTERNOON

CAB TO Beauchamp Place and **Harrod's** for tea if the ① time is right. I always spend time on the tiny street next door, **Beauchamp Place.** It is filled with charming ② little shops and good restaurants. I usually stop in the Map House to poke around.

I then work my way by foot or cab to **Kensington** ③ **Gardens** and the **Albert Memorial.** I love this ornate, overblown, romantic and corny memorial of a queen's ④ love for her husband.

Any time I have left I would spend wandering in this ⑤ garden, up to the **Peter Pan** statue and the Italian Gardens and Queen Anne's alcove. And tea at **The Orangery,** the ⑥ glass house next to Kensington Palace.

EVENING

AN ELEGANT DINNER tonight at **Rule's.** Roast beef and Yorkshire pudding in a place that is over 200 years old. It is really an "old" favorite.

LONDON'S CEMETERIES

A guide to some of the really permanent residents of London

MANY TRAVELERS, including myself, are fascinated by the memorials and burial sites of famous people. London and its environs are filled with such extraordinary places.

If you have been on any of the preceding tours, you will have already visited many such sites including:

Westminster Abbey with its royal tombs, Poets' Corner, the site of the Unknown Soldier and dozens of other monuments, **The Tower of London** and the burial sites for Anne Boleyn and poor little Lady Jane Grey who died at age 16 after ruling England for only nine days; **St. Paul's Cathedral** and its memorials for such greats as the architect Christopher Wren and the poet John Donne.

And memorials in almost every church or churchyard you have visited.

In addition there are many cemeteries in and around London.

BUNHILL FIELDS lies just north of St. Paul's Cathedral with the John Wesley Chapel alongside. Since these fields were unconsecrated ground, you will find many religious dissenters such as Quakers and Baptists.

In addition, Bunhill (from the words Bone Hill) contains bodies from the charnel house which was connected to St. Paul's churchyard. In 1666, the year of the great plague, more than 120,000 bodies were buried here.

Among the famous buried here are Isaac Watts, writer of such hymns as *Joy to the World* and *O God, Our Help in Ages Past;* a memorial to John Bunyan of *Pilgrim's Progress* fame; Daniel Defoe, writer of *Robinson Crusoe* and *Moll Flanders a*nd the artist, poet and painter William Blake.

Others include Susannah Wesley, mother of Methodist reformers John and Charles, and the embezzler, Henry Fauntleroy.

ON THE FAR SOUTHWEST CORNER of London proper you will find the 39-acre **Brompton Cemetery**. Although you will not see very many famous names here, the cemetery is filled with extraordinary monuments, some designated national treasures.

Among the most unusual is the marker for Major Ronald Erne with a little boy and girl in 1920s dress, including knee socks, a sailor's shirt and cap on the boy and anklets, a large hairbow and a dress with a lace collar on the little girl.

A tall monument honors 2,625 pensioners of the Royal Hospital, Chelsea, including a roaring lion. Other monuments honor soldiers of World War I and earlier conflicts.

Look for Frederick Leyland's monument created by the artist Edward Burne-Jones, with beautiful examples of pre-Raphaelite sculpture. Leyland was a patron of the arts.

A monument to Flight Sub-Lieutenant Reginald Alexander John Warneford who destroyed a zeppelin airship in 1915 shows a zeppelin sinking with flames coming out the top and in the corner a small airplane.

The perimeter of the cemetery's great circle contains catacombs with black iron gates.

There is even an American buried here, Blanche Roosevelt, who was the first American woman to sing Italian opera at Covent Garden. Her full-length statue shows her clutching a rose.

Each visitor to this cemetery will come away with

their personal favorite. I guess mine is the one of John Jackson, the fighter, with a gentle-looking lion.

NORTH OF LONDON in Hampstead is the famous **Highgate Cemetery.** Unfortunately, because it was allowed to deteriorate, the West Cemetery at Highgate was closed in 1975. It is currently under renovation and can be visited only by a guided tour, led by one of the Friends of the Cemetery.

The East Cemetery is open to the public. Here you can visit the memorial to George Eliot (Mary Ann Evans) who wrote *Adam Bede, The Mill on the Floss, Silas Marner* and *Middlemarch.*

Look for the great metal bust of Karl Marx, writer of the *Communist Manifesto* across from the plain gray granite memorial sarcophagus with the ashes of Herbert Spencer, the great English philosopher.

Check the area around Dog's Head path, probably overgrown with spring and/or summer flowers. Look for the sculpture of a dog's head with its floppy ears and leather collar.

On the main road you will find the strange stone piano memorializing Harry Thornton, a concert pianist who entertained troops during World War I. Along the road is a relief of five young angel faces and the memorial for Sir Ralph Richardson, the great English actor who died in 1983.

THERE ARE MANY MORE CEMETERIES and memorial sites to visit. But I am only going to mention one more. And for this you really need a car. The famous memorial to the explorer Richard Burton is in the western suburb of Mortlake at **St. Mary Magdalene** (the Catholic church, not the cemetery or the Protestant church.)

Here you will find the famous stone tent: 12 feet square and 18 feet high. Inside are two coffins for Burton and his wife Isabel. He had wanted to be buried in a Bedouin tent; Isabel agreed. Only she had it made of

English marble, instead of canvas.

To properly appreciate this extraordinary memorial, I suggest you do your homework and learn something about this traveler, writer, archeologist, soldier and womanizer.

Enjoy visiting these last resting places of the great and famous and the not-so-famous.

GLOSSARY
OF TERMS

A few hints that will help you understand
our English friends more easily

Biscuit: A cookie if sweet, a cracker if unsweetened
Black or white: With or without cream in coffee
Book: Make a reservation
Chemist: Druggist
Coach: A bus
Dress circle: Mezzanine in a theatre
Ground floor: First floor
First Floor: Second floor
Interval: Intermission at the theatre or concert
Jumper: A sweater
Lift: An elevator
Lorry: A truck
Pub: A bar or tavern
Queue: Waiting line
Return ticket: A round trip ticket
Ring up: Call on the telephone
Single ticket: One way ticket
Stalls: Orchestra seats in a theatre
Upper circle: First balcony in a theatre
Vest: Undershirt
Tube: Subway or underground
Water closet: Toilet

FOOD

Food and drink have their own vocabulary in London. Here are some foods which you will find all over town:

Bangers and mash: Sausages and mashed potato

Bubble and squeak: Cabbage and potato fried with yesterday's roast.

Crumpets: Similar to an English muffin with larger air holes

Fish and chips: Usually cod, plaice or skate served with French-fried potatoes and served with vinegar and salt

Jellied eel: You don't want to know. It looks and tastes just the way it sounds. A Cockney favorite.

Ploughman's lunch: Cheddar cheese, bread, pickled onions and bitters.

Scotch eggs: Hard-boiled eggs encased in sausage and bread crumbs and deep fried.

Shepherd's pie: Diced meat, sometimes with onion and vegetable, covered with mashed potato.

Whitebait: Tiny little whole fish, deep fried.

DRINK

Bitter: Amber-colored draft beer

Cider: Strong fermented apple juice

Light ale: Fizzy beer

Shandy: Bitters with lemonade or ginger beer. Good in the summer.

Stout: Strong, dark and rich ale.

INDEX

MY LONDON

NOTES
&
PLANNER

_____

_____

_____

_____

_____

_____

_____

ABOUT THE AUTHOR

World-traveler Ruth Humleker has been a museum administrator, art fund director, consultant to city and art organizations, Peace Corps teacher in Yemen, and an inveterate traveler. She is also the author of *New York for the Independent Traveler.*